PULLMAN

Also by Julian Morel

Progressive Catering (Caxton)
Scientific Catering & Hotel Operating (Pitman)
Contemporary Catering (Barrie & Jenkins)
At Your Service (Educational Explorers)
Caterer's Companion (Pitman)
Handbook of Wines & Beverages (Pitman)

PULLMAN

The Pullman Car Company — its services, cars, and traditions

Julian Morel

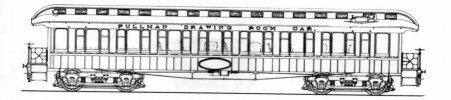

David & Charles
Newton Abbot   London   North Pomfret (Vt)

British Library Cataloguing in Publication Data

Morel, Julian
  The Pullman Car Company.
  1. Pullman Car Company – History
  2. Railways – Great Britain – Pullman cars
  I. Title
  385'.33   T J603.4.G72P/

  ISBN 0–7153–8382–5

Photoset in Plantin by
Northern Phototypesetting Co, Bolton,
and printed in Great Britain by
Redwood Burn Ltd, Trowbridge, Wilts,
for David & Charles (Publishers) Limited
Brunel House, Newton Abbot, Devon

Published in the United states of America
by David & Charles Inc
North Pomfret, Vermont 05053, USA

Contents

'IMPROVEMENT IS OUR WATCHWORD'
George Mortimer Pullman (1831–97)

'PULLMAN & PERFECTION'
Lord Dalziel of Wooler (1854–1927)

'OUR WORK IS BY NO MEANS FINISHED, IT HAS ONLY
JUST BEGUN'
Georges Nagelmackers (1845–1905)

'EVERY DIFFICULTY PRESENTS AN OPPORTUNITY'
Stanley Adams (1892–1965)

Foreword

by Sir John Elliot MInstT

WHEN Pullman cars started to disappear from Britain's crack trains it was a sad day for the discriminating public who had for years enjoyed their unique personal service, and the dedicated and highly trained staff who were proud to wear the Pullman insignia on their jackets.

Mr Morel, who was catering manager to the end under the distinguished direction of Mr Frank Harding, in these pages has made a valuable addition to the railway archives of the period; future transport historians will not fail to take note of the result of his careful researches into the story of this famous old company, and readers today will re-live happy memories of rail travel at its luxurious best.

As Pullman's last chairman I am happy to pay my tribute to him and his colleagues in all departments of a notable public service.

Great Easton   John Elliot
Dunmow
Essex

Introduction

ON a hot summer's afternoon one of the attractions arousing curiosity at Horsted Keynes station on the Bluebell Railway was an old Pullman car named *Fingall*. Built in 1914 the car had seen service on British Railways until 1963 when it was sold to the National Motor Museum. It remained at Beaulieu in Hampshire as a static display with a Schools class engine and two other Pullman cars *Agatha* and No 35, until the late 1970s, eventually finding its way on to the Bluebell Railway in West Sussex. By then the car was very delapidated from neglect, and ravaged by the elements. Yet *Fingall* stood there proudly, patiently awaiting renovation. The car will live again, for it is scheduled for restoration into full running order. Among the spectators that afternoon at Horsted Keynes was a lady and her small son who had obviously asked his mother 'what is a Pullman car'? 'It is', came the succinct reply, 'a carriage you sit down in to have a meal on a train'.

Though a good reply, there is far more to it than that, for the story of Pullman is considerable and comprehensive and goes back a long way in time. But what is a Pullman car? The *Pocket Oxford Dictionary* defines a Pullman as 'a railway saloon carriage'. *Chambers Twentieth Century Dictionary* says a Pullman car is 'a railway sleeping or sitting room car, first made by George Mortimer Pullman (born 1831) in America', whereas the *Oxford Illustrated Dictionary* says, 'type of comfortable railway carriage with fitted tables on which refreshments can be placed (GMP 1831–97) American designer'.

So we are informed the vehicle comes from America, was originally a sleeping or a saloon railway carriage or car and is named after the person who designed/invented it. Now, well over a century since the inception, is a growing interest in and a correlation between Pullman cars and steam traction. Both are passing, or have passed, into railway history to become active subjects for preservation. Is it a mere coincidence that *Fingall* and Richard Maunsell's SR 4–4–0 No 928 *Stowe*, which both stood at Beaulieu, are now reunited on the Bluebell Railway?

Not far from Sheffield Park and Horsted Keynes stations on the Bluebell Line is the Kent & East Sussex Railway at Tenterden, Kent, where steam and three more original Pullman cars are preserved, *Barbara, Cumbria* and *Theodora*. Further afield is the famous railway steam centre and museum at Carnforth in Lancashire where vintage rolling stock, including Pullman cars, is restored and displayed and where charter tours are organised in conjunction with British Rail.

In the United Kingdom there are some 50 railway steam centres and about 100 preserved Pullman cars of which about a half are at present in running order. Many of these vehicles are privately owned. In their heyday on British Railways, steam locomotives were numbered in thousands but Pullman cars were calculated in hundreds, and even then not all were locomotive-hauled. Thus a much higher percentage of Pullman cars has been preserved than steam locomotives! There were electric Pullman trains and others associated with diesel multiple-units. The majority of cars that escaped the breaker's yard are termed locomotive-hauled, be the original motive power diesel, electric or steam. The revival of Pullman prompted this book.

I do, however, claim a special interest in the subject for I served Pullman in Britain for 21 years almost to the day. At Pullman we were encouraged to learn the history of our heritage. During my time with Pullman I kept a diary and collected a mass of paperwork. It forms the nucleus of this book. To the best of my knowledge it is the first and may possibly be the last time a book on Pullman has been written by what I was, and am proud to be, a Pullman man. I hasten to add that I do not write just for myself but also on behalf of those with whom it was a privilege to serve. At Pullman the *esprit-de-corps* was strong and enduring.

When this work was in its planning stage I searched for a

suitable introductory sentiment. I found one in a book entitled *Firing Days* (Oxford Publishing Company) by Harold Gasson. Described as 'the reminiscences of a Great Western fireman', I was very taken by the words the author selected to conclude his story because it reflects my own sentiments in presenting this work on Pullman.

'Regrets? There were many but if I have in this book recaptured some of the atmosphere of Great Western Steam, then all is not lost'.

I hope this work of mine recaptures something of the tradition of service that was always Pullman. If it does then it too has achieved its objective. It all began with one man, George Mortimer Pullman.

Frant,   Julian Morel
East Sussex.

1 George Mortimer Pullman

GEORGE MORTIMER PULLMAN was born on 3 March 1831 at Brocton, New York State, the third of ten children. His father is described as a general mechanic, reputed to be a good job, but with so large a family money was tight and the children had to pull their weight in helping their parents run the household. Proficient in the skills of reading, writing and arithmetic young George Pullman left school at 14 and got himself a job as a clerk in a farm supply store. His salary was the prodigious sum of £20 a year and he remained there for three. From the farm shop he went into business with one of his brothers who was a cabinet maker. This proved to be interesting but unremunerative and at 22, restless and ambitious, he moved to Chicago and worked as a building contractor. Young Pullman had a good head for business and in the land of free enterprise and competition and in the city he grew to love, began to do well and earn money. Around this time he met and married Hattie Sanger, a Chicago girl.

Legend has it that on their honeymoon the newly weds travelled overnight by train from Buffalo to Westfield, a distance of 58 miles, in a sleeping car. It was an uncomfortable journey. Dissatisfied with the crude accommodation and unable to sleep, Pullman spent the night thinking how the vehicle in which they were travelling could be improved. The idea of the car, which was to bear his name, was born.

It will be noted Mr and Mrs Pullman were travelling in a sleeping car, so it would not be true to say he invented this type of vehicle. Sleeping cars appeared on American railroads some 20 years before Pullman's famous overnight trip between Buffalo and Westfield. The first two roads, it is claimed, to introduce sleeping cars were the Cumberland Valley Railroad in 1836, followed in 1843 by the New York & Erie Railroad. Pullman tried to sell his idea of a superior type of car to the railway company. It was turned down on the familiar pretext — even in those days — as being 'uneconomic', and the railway was quite content with its existing arrangements. Pullman decided to go it alone. He purchased a day coach from the Chicago & Alton Railroad and with the assistance of Leonard Seibert, a skilled cabinet maker he had met in Chicago, converted car No 9 into a sleeper. Pullman persuaded the C&A to run it and it went into traffic in 1859 between Bloomington and Chicago on the Alton road. It is on record that J. L. Barnes, the first Pullman conductor, stated that his most difficult task was persuading male passengers to remove their footwear before getting into the bunks. They seemed afraid to take their boots off.

Barnes did not wear a uniform, just a badge. A supplementary charge was paid to Pullman by the passengers for the use of the car; the railroad took the basic fare. The venture proved a moderate success and two other cars followed, Nos 12 and 19. In a short space of time Pullman and his associates converted, owned and operated a small fleet of 12 cars. Encouraged, Pullman wanted to convert more cars and improve upon the existing designs, but lacked the capital. The railway was still reluctant to back him financially. He had to seek the money elsewhere. Pullman saw an opportunity in the Colorado Pike's Peak or Bust gold rush. He moved to a Colorado mining town and opened a trading store selling supplies to the prospectors. This proved to be far more consistent and profitable than the more precarious function of digging for gold. With the money acquired he returned to Chicago and at his own expense built his first car which he aptly name *Pioneer*. It was a magnificent and opulent vehicle admired by all who saw it; unfortunately it was out of loading gauge for many of the platforms and bridges on the Chicago & Alton Railroad. It became known as Pullman's Folly. By this time he had spent all his capital and was about to turn his back upon railroads when a tragic twist of fate came to the rescue.

In April 1865 President Abraham Lincoln was assassinated, and his body was being taken by special train to Springfield, his birthplace, for burial. The stops en-route were frequent, memorial services were held for those who wished to pay their last respects to their dead President, and by the time the *cortége* reached Chicago Mrs Lincoln collapsed. Arrangements had to be made for her return direct to Springfield and Pullman promptly offered his car. This time the railway had little option but to accept. An army of workmen was dispatched to alter the necessary platforms and bridges to allow the car to pass and the funeral special including *Pioneer* left Chicago for Springfield on 2 May 1865.

Overnight *Pioneer*, the first Pullman car, became famous. General Ulysses Grant succeeded Lincoln and the new President used the car afterwards on a journey to Detroit, his home town, and again to make this possible platforms and bridges on the Chicago & North Western Railroad had to be altered. Pullman's reputation was established by these dramatic events, ample capital became available, no time was lost in building new cars and within gauge, and from that moment he never looked back. The original Pullman car was not a diner nor a saloon, nor parlour, but a sleeping car. Pullman did not invent the sleeping car, but improved upon the idea by providing superior accommodation. He was an innovator. His slogan was 'Improvement is our watchword' and he practised what he preached.

His first contract was with the Chicago & Alton Railroad to build and operate sleeping cars on the system; contracts with other roads followed. After *Pioneer* six cars were built: *Atlantic, Aurora, City of Chicago, Maritana, Omaha* and *Pacific*. The naming of the cars followed the practice of the stagecoach. Pullman's formula was quite simple. He would provide and staff the cars, in return the railway would haul and maintain them from the floor down. The railway would collect the fares and Pullman obtain his revenue by raising an extra charge – the Pullman supplement – on the passengers for the use of the cars. Later when catering was introduced this provided additional revenue. This formula was so successful that it remained virtually unchanged for over 100 years. It was adopted in Britain by Pullman and by the Wagons-Lits organisation on mainland Europe although W-L also maintained under-floor gear.

Until this time it was the practice in the USA as well as in Britain and elsewhere, on long journeys to stop the train at suitable points to allow passengers to buy food and drink in the station refreshment room. This frequently delayed the train and usually entailed an indignified scramble for the unfortunate passengers, who were in any case often segregated by class of travel. The system was also open to abuse, and collusion between unscrupulous catering contractors and railway staff was rife. When this happened the passengers were harried by the blowing of whistles and shouts of 'all aboard' leaving scant time to consume the food and drink already paid for. This somewhat comical situation was a popular subject for cartoonists and other wits of the period. The experienced and the more prosperous travellers, in order to avoid the station stampede, would bring their own food and drink with them in expensive, well appointed and fashionable en-route or travelling baskets. Some roads also featured a service of meal baskets which could be ordered in advance and were supplied by contractors along the line. The rush for refreshments, the indifferent and varying standards of station food and meal baskets with the resultant digestive and other troubles and complaints of the long suffering passengers all contributed to the hazards of early rail travel. But it did much more than that, for it gave railway catering the indelible mediocre image which has so ruthlessly and relentlessly pursued it down the years to this very day and from which it just cannot escape, try as it may.

The problems of feeding passengers at whistle stops did not escape the alert and enterprising George Mortimer Pullman. He identified an additional source of revenue. Why not feed the passengers on-board the train? Characteristically he introduced the hotel car, so called because it offered the same service as an hotel – somewhere to sleep, sit and to eat. The car was a sleeper in which the top berths folded away, tables were fitted between the lower ones and meals were served from a kitchen positioned at one end of the vehicle. The first hotel cars were *City of Boston*, *City of New York*, *Kalamazoo*, *President* and *Western World*. Car *President* went into traffic on the Great Western Railroad of Canada, the first Pullman to operate outside the USA. In 1868 Pullman introduced his first dining car, the garish and sumptuously decorated *Delmonico*, named after the world famous New York restaurant, which ran on the Chicago & Alton. The name of the car gives an indication as to the standard of service aspired. It will be noted that the dining car came later than the sleeper but more significant still, to enable passengers to reach this vehicle, it brought about the introduction of corridors and vestibules.

Noting the growing Pullman fleet and the contracts he acquired, and with other sleeping cars on the American roads before the advent of Pullman, competitors were inevitable. But Pullman always managed to keep the initiative. In time he was able to buy out the competition and merge their works and building facilities with his own. One particular rival, the Wagner Palace Car Company, founded by a railway engineer contemporary, Walter Wagner, he was never able to acquire. It was only three years after Pullman died that the two organisations, of necessity, finally merged.

Pullman was successful because he was better than his competitors. Not just the cars, but the on-board service, and most of all his organisation was more efficient. The cars were better built, the heating and lighting arrangements, the furnishings, appointments and ambience all superior. But Pullman was shrewd enough to know that providing fine cars was one thing and the provision of an attentive and courteous service on-board was something else. This was the all important human element and so the travelling staff were carefully selected and trained. The job security offered, the pay and prestige made Pullman employment very attractive. The original train crews were recruited from newly freed slaves, blacks who had been in service as butlers, house boys, attendants and cooks. They were excellent material from which The Pullman Porter became a

George Mortimer Pullman

A standard Pullman dining car Bill-of-Fare
circa 1868

MENU

OYSTERS

Raw	.50
Fried or Roast	.60

COLD

Beef, Tongue, Sugar-Cured Ham.	.40
Pressed Corn Beef, Sardines.	.40
Chicken Salad, Lobster Salad.	.40

BROILED

Beefsteak, with Potatoes.	.60
Mutton Chop, with Potatoes.	.60
Ham, with Potatoes.	.40

EGGS

Boiled, Fried, Scrambled, Omelette Plain.	.40
Omelette with Rum.	.50

—CHOW CHOW PICKLES—

Welsh Rarebit	.50
French Coffee	.25
Tea	.25

Note: Prices are in American cents.

national institution in America. Pullman was particularly meticulous in his management selection, recruiting only the best. He headed a management team consisting of experts in all their respective fields. He was a realist and disliked 'Yes men'. Whether in North America, in Europe or elsewhere the Pullman image is one of quality, efficiency and service to the travelling public.

The Pullman organisation was built on a solid business

foundation and he proved that people were prepared to pay for the best. Quality is remembered long after price is forgotten. But Pullman, as we know, did not have it all his own way, for he operated in a highly competitive market. One particular competitor, in the early days, was the redoubtable Scottish-born financier, Andrew Carnegie, then with the Pennsylvania Railroad. For a while both men opposed each other in veiled hostility over a coveted contract on the Union Pacific Railroad, the largest system in the West. One evening, quite by chance they came face to face in the St Nicholas Hotel, New York, where they were both staying. Though they had met briefly on previous occasions, they were not well acquainted. It was Carnegie who broke the ice and the two men got talking, dined together and by the end of the evening decided to pool resources. An agreement was signed, the Pullman Palace Car Company was formed and Pullman with the backing of Carnegie became a millionaire at the age of 38.

Bill-of-Fare featured on hotel car *President* 1867.

Prairie Chicken	*$1.00*
Woodcock	*$1.00*
Pheasant	*$1.00*
Snipe, Quail, Golden Plover	
Blue Winged Teal, Each	*.75*
Cold Tongue, Ham & Corned Beef	*.30*
Venison	*.60*
Chicken, Whole	*.75*
Half Chicken	*.50*
Sirloin Steak	*.50*
Sardines, Lobster & Broiled Ham or Bacon	*.40*

'while game is plentiful in the West, the Pullmans, with their facilities, are able to make a bill-of-fare and serve it in a style which would cause Delmonico to wring his hands in anguish. The service is on the European plan; that is you pay for what you order'.

Acknowledgement: *The Newcomen Society in North America. (1951).*

The Wagner Palace Car Company has already been mentioned and it is interesting to note the use of the word *Palace*. This was the Victorian era when kings and queens, emperors, czars and mikados had great influence and power in world affairs, even in republican America. Every city had a Palace Hotel and its quota of palatial mansions. Naming the company with the inclusion of the term *Palace* would prove alluring to travellers. Besides, Pullman, like Wagner and others, was in what we now define as the up-market. The first Pullman works were established at Elmira, New York; Detroit, Michigan; and St Louis, Missouri. But with an ever increasing demand for sleeping, parlour, restaurant and other types of cars, as well as for passenger and freight rolling stock, further engineering, maintenance and building facilities were required. Pullman decided to build a works in Chicago, the city he now regarded as his home town and which was fast becoming the railroad centre of the USA. In 1880 he purchased a site of 3,500 acres by Lake Calumet some 14 miles to the south of the city. The land was a prairie and first had to be drained; on it Pullman built a model town for his workers and a works which incorporated the very latest ideas in engineering design. Here was introduced for the first time an assembly line production unit capable of building a variety of Pullman cars, railway, street and freight vehicles. Pullman City grew to a town of 12,000 inhabitants with its own shopping centre, schools, bank, church, theatre, hotel, parks and pleasure areas. There were the huge construction shops dominated by a great clock tower, the yards, workers' dwellings, and horse drawn trams; even the public works belonged to the company. It was a prosperous community and a genuine attempt at a welfare state. In 1893 the United States ran into financial difficulties and the resultant national recession caused a widespread industrial slump. Production was reduced at Pullman City and wages had to be cut. George Pullman was in a dilemma; on the one hand he had shareholders to pacify and on the other a work-force to protect. He acted in all good faith. But there was an undercurrent of unrest in the city emanating from a minority who objected to having their lives regulated by the company. This now came out into the open and caused a series of strikes which culminated into the famous Pullman riots and the blacking, by the American Railway Union, of all Pullman cars and movement of mail and freight. Alarmed by a deteriorating situation President Grover Cleveland dispatched Federal troops to Pullman City. Order had to be restored by force of arms and Eugene Dobs, the union leader who led the strikers, was jailed for six months. The strike was broken but in the inquiry which followed, the Pullman Company was ordered to dispose of all property forthwith not used or intended for industrial purposes, and Pullman City was annexed to Chicago.

George Pullman never fully recovered from the failure of his City; it was a bitter disappointment, and a serious set-back. His life was not all success and he had his failures, the two biggest being the Pullman City débacle and the inability to extend his activities on to the Continent of Europe, beyond a foothold in Italy, for the Wagons-Lits organisation was too strongly established. Here he had to contend with the Belgian head of Wagons-Lits, Georges Nagelmackers who was reluctant to deal with Pullman and anyway did not lack financial support.

Pullman was not a hard but an efficient worker, dividing his time between his offices in Chicago and New York. When out of the office he would tour the country in his private car PPC built at Detroit in 1877. PPC stood for the President's Private Car, the President in this case being Pullman. When not in use, the car, complete with staff, was available for hire. After Pullman's death the car was renamed *Monitor* and continued in traffic until 1921. During its 44 years' service the car had conveyed all the Presidents of the United States of America in that period.

The name Pullman was to be commemorated in two vehicles. In 1933 the first aluminium lightweight sleeping car was named *George M Pullman*. In 1981 the last rail-passenger vehicle to come out of the Chicago works before it closed down was similarly named. The second *George M Pullman* was built for AMTRAK, (The National Railroad Passenger Corporation) completing an order for its Superliner fleet in which it carries AMTRAK fleet number 32009.

19

Long before the development of the motor car and the coming of the airways the private rail car was a regular feature of American railroad travel. Between 300 and 400 were outshopped by Pullman and either privately owned or leased out on hire fully staffed. These cars were the most lavishly decorated and luxuriously appointed of all Pullmans. The age of the private car is described in Lucius Beebe's profusely illustrated classic *Mansions on Rails*. The famous work is of prime interest since it is devoted almost entirely to Pullman. The work is based upon files and photographs long forgotten and discovered in the Pullman archives in Chicago. The reader is left in wonderment at the luxury, opulence and colourful liveries of those private cars and no less at the wealth of their owners.

Opinions differ as to the character of George Mortimer Pullman the man. What was he like as a person? Here the author was fortunate to have known in 1951 an American, Edgar Mayer, who had settled in England with his wife, and was a shareholder of the Pullman Car Company Limited. During the last seven years of the life of George M. Pullman, Edgar Mayer was his personal secretary. He lived with the Pullman family in their spacious mansion in fashionable Prairie Avenue, Chicago and travelled everywhere with his master. At that time there were four children – two daughters and two sons – none of whom followed in their father's footsteps. Mrs Pullman was described as an invalid. George Pullman, according to Edgar Mayer, was a difficult man, hard in business but always straight, scrupulously fair and most honourable in all his dealings. He was particularly proud of his humble beginnings of which he would often speak. Discussing the Pullman riots, Edgar Mayer confirmed the great man's disappointment. He never got over it. Edgar Mayer was also able to throw new light on the cause of the Pullman riots. The real cause of the trouble came not from within, for the Pullman employees were generally loyal to the Company, but from subversive outside elements and vested interests in gambling saloons and brothels which Pullman, a religious man, would not allow within the precincts of the City. As a young man Edgar Mayer had numerous happy recollections of the Pullman *ménage.* Pullman was particularly fond of his grandson George Mortimer Pullman Lowden, the son of the man destined to become Governor of Illinois, and Pullman's daughter Florence, Mrs Frank O. Lowden.

Pullman died suddenly of a heart attack aged 66 on 19 October, 1897. Four days later he was laid to rest at Graceland Cemetery, Chicago. His premature death stunned America. To Edgar Mayer's great surprise Pullman, in his will, left him a legacy of $10,000. 'He never praised me, but he must have been pleased with my services for this was a very generous token of his gratitude.' After his death Pullman was succeeded by Robert T. Lincoln, son of the late President, as head of the Pullman Company; the *Palace* had been dropped, and the organisation continued to develop and build as well as operate its cars. In 1927 the organisation became Pullman Incorporated with two subsidiaries, the Pullman Company as the operating side and Pullman Standard Car Manufacturing Company, the building component. By the mid-1930s a fleet of 8,500 cars operated in North America. There were 1,400 services and 30,000 employees were on the payroll. The fleet was made up of parlour and sleeping cars; restaurant, club, observation, and private cars, and brakes.

The construction side of the business had long since extended its range outside all forms of passenger vehicles to freight cars, trams, buses, trailers for lorries, track maintenance machines and to boats. Six great Pullman Standard works handled the construction side at Bessemer, Alabama; Worcester, Massachusetts; Michigan City and Hammond, Indiana; Butler, Pennsylvania and the original shops at Chicago, Illinois. George Mortimer Pullman might not have recognised his original company but his spirit of enterprise and improvement lived on. It had also fulfilled his ambition of a monopoly. In 1940, inspired by a construction competitor, the US Government brought a suit against Pullman Incorporated under the Sherman Anti-Trust Law claiming an unlawful monopoly had been created. They were given the choice either to build or to operate, but they could not do both. Pullman Incorporated selected the construction side and the building of cars became divorced from operation.

However, as Pullman Incorporated was at the time on essential war work this parting of the ways – construction and operation – did not become wholly operative until 1947 when the Pullman Company was bought out by a consortium of 59 American railroads. Carroll Rede Harding from the Southern Pacific, who had played a leading role in the purchasing negotiations, was elected its president and the Pullman Company continued to operate as previously, as a concessionaire, for a further 21 years. In the 1970s, with the recession hitting the American railroads, AMTRAK, together with the other roads, assumed the responsibility for catering and all other on-board services. In 1979, Pullman Incorporated, the original company, now an even more diversified enterprise with 14 plants in the USA and in Canada, announced that no more Pullman cars would be built by its Pullman-Standard Corporation subsidiary. Since the railway passenger car side of the business at Chicago and at Hammond was no longer financially viable it was closed. 1980/1 marked the end of the Pullman car in the USA after some 112 years' service.

2 Pullman Comes to Britain

THE fame of George Mortimer Pullman and the success of his cars spread to Europe. Many visitors were attracted to the USA and two in particular need a special mention. One was the founder of the Compagnie Internationale des Wagons-Lits (CIWL), a Belgian engineer by the name of Georges Nagelmackers (1845–1905) who visited the United States in 1868. The other was Sir James Allport, general manager of the Midland Railway from 1857 to 1879 who toured America in 1872, travelled extensively in Pullman cars and met their creator in Chicago.

Suitably impressed, Sir James invited George Pullman to London where on 18 February, 1873 he addressed a Midland Railway shareholders' meeting. It resulted in a neat 15-year contract with the Midland to supply and operate, without any cost to the railway, which would get the fares, as many sleeping, parlour and dining cars as the demand warranted. At the same time Pullman would be free to negotiate contracts with other railway companies in Britain.

The cars would be built at the Pullman shops in Detroit, shipped over in sections to the Midland's works at Derby where they would be assembled. The first cars, *Midland, Excelcior* and *Enterprise* were sleepers, *Victoria* and *Britannia* were drawing room, or parlour cars. They started operating out of St Pancras on 1 June 1874 as an all-Pullman train to Bradford; the following year a Pullman train operated between St Pancras and Liverpool. By 1876, after two years' operation, 36 cars were in service on the Midland extending from St Pancras to Bradford, Liverpool, Leeds, Manchester and through to Scotland by the newly opened Settle & Carlisle line to Glasgow and Edinburgh.

They worked though as single cars rather than complete trains since the original Bradford service was not a success. Moreover the cars were parlours for day service and sleepers by night. Meal service was not included; diners were a later development.

The standard of comfort and the appointments of the cars was matched only by the quality of the on-board service. The cars' staff were recruited exclusively from private service, a policy which was to persist right up to the second world war. In the manner of the American company, car staff were known then as porters, not attendants; this name came later. A conductor was always in charge of a service and was responsible for collecting the supplement fares and checking the Pullman tickets.

The British Pullman Palace Car Company was registered on 2 June 1882, as a subsidiary of the American company, with George Mortimer Pullman as chairman. Meanwhile he had been far from idle and other contracts were negotiated in Britain and in Italy. In 1875 an office was opened in Milan and works acquired in Turin where American-built cars were assembled, while others shipped over from Britain were modified. By 1876 a fleet of 20 Pullman sleepers was working on Italian railways. These cars were a thorn in Nagelmackers' side, with whom Pullman was unable to do business. It is said Pullman's price was too high – he wanted control of Wagons-Lits. Nothing came of the protracted negotiations, and in 1888 Pullman sold out to Nagelmackers who added the Italian cars and the works to his empire. In the fullness of time Italy became a large and important division of CIWL with headquarters in Rome and works at Milan as well as in the Italian capital. Pullman cars were always popular in Italy but some 37 years were to pass before they ran again on Italian metals.

The 97 year Pullman association with the Brighton line commenced in 1875 and lasted until 1972. The original cars were transferred from the Midland Railway to operate on the London, Brighton & South Coast Railway. Later Detroit and Pullman City built cars were shipped in sections direct for assembly at Brighton railway works. Not to be outdone by the Midland, the Great Northern Railway negotiated a contract with Pullman for sleeping and other cars and on 1 November, 1879 a notable event occurred when a Pullman dining car *Prince of Wales* went into traffic between Kings Cross and Leeds. Meals had been served previously on Midland cars, but this was the first regular dining service with meals prepared and cooked on board and the forerunner of on-train catering on British railways, with Pullman blazing the trail. The American-built car was originally the parlour *Ohio*, converted and renamed at Derby for the Great Northern Railway. The car went into service on the 10.00 from Leeds, arriving at Kings Cross at 14.00, returning from London at 17.30. Before going into regular service there were two demonstration trips for the press from Kings Cross to Peterborough on 17 October, 1879, and from Leeeds ten days later.

The Pullman conductor was James Bower from Portsmouth who at 14 ran away to sea. He was to settle in Chicago where he joined the Pullman Palace Car Company and worked as a conductor on many roads. In 1877 he returned to England with George Pullman and served on the Midland and then on the GNR. One hundred years on, in 1979, British Rail and Travellers-Fare combined to celebrate the centenary of on-train catering. A Centenary Express, made up of preserved cars from the National Railway Museum, York, toured the Regions of British Rail for static displays as well as demonstration trips. Included in the formation of this special were three Pullman cars: *Eagle*, *Emerald II* and *Topaz 1*. James Bower's grandson Anthony Bower, a schoolteacher from Solihull, was invited by Travellers-Fare to travel on the press run of the Centenary Express on 13 September 1979. Moreover he was able to clarify some of the events of 1879 from family papers.

By 1880 Pullman cars were operating on the Midland, London Brighton & South Coast, London & South Western, Highland, and then on the London, Chatham & Dover railways. In 1888 the Midland contracts expired and were not renewed. The Pullman cars were bought by the railway to be operated by the newly formed Midland hotel services under the able direction of William Towle, later to become Sir William Towle. His sons also had railway connections – one on the LMS itself succeeding his father, the other as chairman of Gordon Hotels involved in railway catering. Towards the turn of the century the railway companies were entering the field of hotels and catering with the exception of those which in 1923 formed the Southern Railway. They kept their catering out to contract. The firms involved at varying times were Spiers & Pond, J. Lyons & Company, Frederick Hotels, Gordon Hotels, Bertram, and the Pullman Car Company.

In 1907, financier Davison Alexander Dalziel (1854–1927) later to become Sir Davison and then Lord Dalziel of Wooler, purchased the British Pullman Car Company. In 1915 the Pullman Car Company was formed to take over Dalziel's interests and nominated him as chairman. The assets included a fleet of 74 cars and contracts with the London Brighton & South Coast, South Eastern & Chatham, Caledonian, and Metropolitan railways, though some of the contracts were in abeyance for the duration of the 1914–18 war. Lord Dalziel had been MP for Brixton, owned a London evening newspaper and introduced taxi cabs to the capital. As a young man he had worked in the USA where he saw something of the railroads and the potential of Pullman car services. From the time he acquired control of the British Pullman Car Company, no more cars were built in the USA for British services and new cars were British-built, the first by Metropolitan Carriage & Wagon Co of Birmingham and Cravens of Sheffield. Lord Dalziel was as astute a businessman as George Pullman himself, and a financier of outstanding ability. He was to develop the Pullman Car Company to serve routes where the traffic was the most remunerative, and insisted on the highest standards of 'Pullman and perfection'. A powerful figure in the City he masterminded the purchase of Thomas Cook & Son, the travel agency, by CIWL forming the Cook/Wagons-Lits organisation with about 400 travel offices worldwide. He was also to control as chairman the famous trio of Thomas Cook, Wagons-Lits and Pullman.

Pullman cars were progressively extended on CIWL services in Italy (where they were more correctly re-introduced), France,

Egypt and elsewhere. The cars were built in Britain, equipped by the Pullman Car Company and sold to CIWL. So close and enduring was the association between Wagons-Lits and Pullman that the similarity of the two organisations and of the cars themselves and their equipment lasted for well over 40 years after the death of Lord Dalziel. This close association may have had something to do with the fact that Lord Dalziel's daughter was married to Nagelmackers' son René.

To the Cook/Wagons-Lits organisation there is a sequel. When France and Belgium fell to German occupation in 1940, Cooks became separated from its CIWL parent and was subsequently taken over by a consortium of the British four main line railway companies. With the nationalisation of the railways in 1948 Thomas Cook & Son passed to public ownership and became a subsidiary of the British Transport Commission. One of Thomas Cook's many interests was a subsidiary, British Holiday Estates Limited, which owned and managed the Farringford Hotel on the Isle of Wight and a holiday camp at Prestatyn in North Wales. The camp was a joint venture with the LMS. Pullman staff were sent from London to assist with the opening arrangements. In more recent years Thomas Cook was denationalised, and is now, as Thomas Cook Ltd, a member of the Midland Bank Group.

Lord Dalziel developed Pullman in Britain principally on the Southern and the Great Eastern with Continental travel connecting London with the Channel and North Sea ports through Newhaven, Folkestone, Dover and Harwich. After his death Dalziel was succeeded as Pullman's chairman by Lord Ashfield (1874–1948), the creator of London Transport, then by Sir Follett Holt KBE and in 1944 by Stanley Adams. In reality the Dalziel mantle, and all his directorships, passed to his former private secretary, Stanley Adams, who had been general manager of Thomas Cook, with seats on the Board of Wagons-Lits and the Pullman Car Company. The Directeur-Générale of Wagons-Lits also had a seat on the Board of Pullman, the last three being Le Comte de Ségur-Lamoignon; Baron R. Snoy and René Margot-Noblemaire. It fell to Stanley Adams to reinstate

PULLMAN
services

MIDLAND PULLMAN
(Diesel-Electric De-Luxe Service)
Manchester Central–Cheadle Heath
St. Pancras
(Daily Services except Saturdays and Sundays)

BIRMINGHAM PULLMAN
(Diesel-Electric De-Luxe Service)
Wolverhampton–Birmingham (Snow Hill)
Leamington Spa–Paddington
(Daily Services except Saturdays and Sundays)

BRISTOL PULLMAN
(Diesel-Electric De-Luxe Service)
Bristol–Bath–Paddington
(Daily Services except Saturdays and Sundays)

SOUTH WALES PULLMAN
Swansea–Neath–Port Talbot–Bridgend
Cardiff–Newport–Paddington
(Daily Services except Saturdays and Sundays)

TEES-TYNE PULLMAN
Newcastle–Darlington–York–King's Cross
(Daily Services except Saturdays and Sundays)

YORKSHIRE PULLMAN
Harrogate–Leeds–Bradford–Wakefield–Hull–Doncaster–King's Cross
(Weekday Service)

MASTER CUTLER
Sheffield (Victoria)–Retford–London
London–Grantham–Peterborough–Retford–Sheffield (Victoria)
(Daily Services except Saturdays and Sundays)

HARROGATE SUNDAY PULLMAN
King's Cross–Leeds–Bradford–Harrogate

QUEEN OF SCOTS PULLMAN
King's Cross–Leeds–Harrogate–Darlington–Newcastle–Edinburgh–Glasgow
(Weekday Service in each direction)

BOURNEMOUTH BELLE
Waterloo–Southampton–Bournemouth Central
(Daily Service)

OCEAN LINER TRAINS
Waterloo–Southampton

GOLDEN ARROW AND CONTINENTAL SERVICES
Via Dover–Folkestone–Newhaven–Southampton
(Daily Service)

SOUTH COAST SERVICES
London–Brighton–Hove
Worthing–Littlehampton–Bognor
Eastbourne–Hastings
(Daily Services)

THE PULLMAN CAR COMPANY LIMITED
167, VICTORIA STREET, LONDON, S.W.1
and at Victoria Station, London, S.W.1.

Pullman services at their zenith listed in the 1962 ABC *Railway Guide*.

the Company at the end of the second world war. In this he was assisted by the dynamic Frank Dryden Moile Harding OBE the general manager. Stanley Adams retired in 1957, he was succeeded by a distinguished railwayman, Sir John Elliot, the last chairman of the Pullman Car Company. At the same time F. D. M. Harding was promoted managing director.

Sir John Elliot is a personality. Onetime public relations officer of the Southern Railway, the first railway PRO, he became, in succession its acting general manager replacing Sir Eustace Missenden; chief regional officer of the Southern and then of London Midland Region; chairman of the Railway Executive of the BTC; chairman of London Transport Executive and finally chairman of Thomas Cook, Pullman and a director of CIWL. Sir John's interests are many. He is an acknowledged authority on Napoleon Bonaparte, military history and the French Revolution about which he wrote a colourful account, *The Way of the Tumbrils*. Appropriately the new chairman's book went on sale in the Trianon Bar of the Golden Arrow. He also wrote racy reviews of books on all these subjects in the *Daily Telegraph*.

Under Stanley Adams, Sir John Elliot and F. D. M. Harding, Pullman grew to its zenith with services on all five BR Regions, works at Preston Park, Brighton, a depot stores at Battersea, administrative offices at Victoria station, and 800 staff on the payroll. Post-war Pullman was promoted by the Company as comfort in travel and for its standard of service rather than associating the image with such terms as luxury or opulence.

Pullman was unaffected by the nationalisation of the railways on 1 January 1948 but in 1954 the British Transport Commission bought out the ordinary shares, giving the BTC control of Pullman. The Company continued to operate separately under its own management, which remained virtually unchanged for the next eight years until the existing contracts ran out. They were not renewed.

On Monday 1 January 1963 Doctor Richard (later Lord) Beeching integrated the Pullman Car Company as a Division of British Transport Hotels. Pullman was now wholly nationalised

PULLMAN CAR COMPANY LIMITED. 1944.

DIRECTORS.

Stanley J. Adams (chairman & managing director)

Richard S. Guinness   The Hon H. E. Fitzalan-Howard[x]

Sir Basil Goulding, Bart.   M. René Margot-Noblemaire[xx]

General Manager   *Secretary*
F. D. M. Harding, OBE   E. J. Morris

Offices of the Company: 10, Mayfair Place, London W1

Notes: [x] became Viscount Fitzalan of Derwent.
       [xx] of CIWL, replaced Baron Robert Snoy.

PULLMAN CAR COMPANY LIMITED. 1962

DIRECTORS

Sir John Elliot. MInstT (chairman & joint managing director)
F. D. M. Harding, OBE MInstT (joint managing director)
M. René Margot-Noblemare.   Guy Lewis Ian McLaren[x]
E. J. Morris. MInstT

Secretary
E. J. Morris

Offices of the Company: 167, Victoria Street, London SW1

Note: [x] joined Board 1954, destined to take over as general manager. Did not materialise for personal reasons.

and responsible to the general manager of BTH. Little more than two months later, on 25 March, a change of top management placed the responsibility for the Pullman Division with the chief of refreshment rooms and restaurant cars of BTH, and, four years later, on 14 March 1967 the Pullman Division was merged into the restaurant car departments of the various BR regions. After 93 years on British railways, Pullman had ceased to be operational as a separate entity, although the Company name survives listed among the BRB subsidiaries at Rail House, Euston. As inspector Wally Cullen, one of the most respected of Pullman members of staff would say 'There was nothing like Pullman'. And Pullman is far from forgotten. In railway literature in just about every book published there is a mention of Pullman. To this day seldom a month passes without one or other of the monthly railway periodicals containing something about Pullman. The Pullman story, though, covers a wide field and with the Wagons-Lits connection the following chapters describe Pullman activities in detail.

3 The Wagons-Lits Company

THE full title of this famous organisation is, or was, *La Compagnie Internationale des Wagons-Lits et des Grands Express Européens.* Today in line with its widespread tourist involvement it is *La Compagnie Internationale des Wagons-Lits et du Tourisme.* We know that Georges Nagelmackers visited the USA, met George Pullman and faced him later as a competitor in Italy and quite possibly in Britain. But the story of Wagons-Lits begins in the USA with one of Pullman's smaller, but none the less active, competitors, Colonel William D'Alton Mann, late of the US Cavalry. The exploits of the gallant Colonel, son of an Ohio farmer, were perhaps not quite with the Seventh Cavalry of movie fame, though he did serve in the Civil War, but allied to rather suspect ventures and shady journalism, before he became interested in the railway sleeping car business. He devised a vehicle which he called a boudoir car, boudoir being defined as a lady's private room. The Colonel's cars were apparently well named; he made some minor progress in the USA and surprisingly enough on the Great Northern and the London, Chatham & Dover Railway in Britain. Whereas Pullman at that time favoured open saloons, the Mann cars were not only more ostentatiously appointed, they were divided into private compartments.

Georges Nagelmackers, son of a Liège banker, shortly after returning from the USA decided to introduce sleeping and other cars based upon the Pullman concept to the principal railways in Europe. He enlisted financial support from his influential father who in turn interested no less a person than King Leopold II of the Belgians (1835–1909) in the project. A company was registered in Liège as Georges Nagelmackers et Cie, contracts

George Mortimer Pullman, 1831–97

One of the pioneer American-built Pullmans in Britain, pre-schedule Midland parlour car No 8 of 1876. (*BR, LMR*)

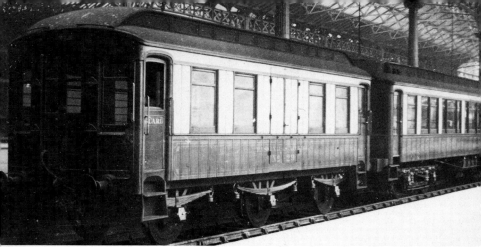

One of the two six-wheel 'Pullman Pups' built with guards and luggage space and a generator to provide electricity for lighting on the 1888 Pullman train on the Brighton line.

Pullman buffet car *Duchess of Norfolk* built in the USA and assembled at Brighton works of the LBSCR in 1906. Note the clerestory roof and the destination board 'Victoria, Hove and West Worthing'. (*Lens of Sutton*)

Twelve-wheel buffet car *Grosvenor*, one of the first British-built cars by Metropolitan C & W Co for the 1908 Southern Belle set.

were negotiated and Nagelmacker's sleepers started to operate on Belgian, French and German railways.

At the outbreak of the Franco-Prussian War of 1870 all operations ceased, contracts lapsed and the Company was forced into suspension. After peace was declared Nagelmackers endeavoured to start again, but the war had dealt him a serious blow and he now was devoid of financial support. It was at this stage that Colonel d'Alton Mann stepped in. Hearing of Nagelmacker's plight a meeting was arranged between them. The Colonel managed to sell him the idea of his boudoir cars and the two men went into partnership. Somehow the Colonel raised the required capital and in 1873 registered Mann's Railway Sleeping Carriage Company Limited (somewhere along the line the boudoir was dropped) and Nagelmackers was back in business.

Contracts with the various railway companies were regenerated and the cars started running again. But the going was hard and things moved too slowly for the restless Colonel who soon tired of his European ventures. He left the running of the Company more and more to his partner. Eventually he sold out to Nagelmackers who managed, through King Leopold II and the assistance of the Belgian government – the issue was now one of national prestige – to raise the necessary capital.

Colonel D'Alton Mann made a killing from the deal and returned to his beloved New York to revive his sleeping and private rail car activities. The return of the Colonel did not worry George Pullman who was now in a very strong position; he merely dealt with him as he was able to do with the majority of competitors, by buying out the Mann organisation in 1889, merging it with his own. Colonel William D'Alton Mann went back to his more profitable and certainly less arduous journalistic activities.

On 14 December 1876 a meeting was held in Brussels comprising members of the proposed Board of the Wagons-Lits company, the creditors and the liquidators of Mann's Railway Sleeping Carriage Company Limited. It was at this meeting the Wagons-Lits Company was formed, registered in Brussels with

Nagelmackers as Administrateur – Directeur-Générale. The '*et des Grands Express Européens*' was added in 1883 when restaurant cars joined the fleet and composite trans-continental *trains-de-luxe* entered service.

The new Company acquired 21 contracts and Wagons-Lits vehicles were operating in Belgium, France, Germany, Austria and Italy. It was in 1883 that the Paris-Constantinople (Istanbul) Orient Express, with a Calais connection, was inaugurated. The same year saw the start of the Calais Mediterranean Express, to the French Riviera, which was to become Le Train Bleu. The Paris-Madrid-Lisbon Sud Express was introduced in 1887, and 12 years later in 1898 the Moscow-Vladivostok Trans-Siberian, followed by the St Petersbourg-Vienna-Cannes Express; by 1899 CIWL had extended its operations to Egypt, Algeria, Tunisia and Morocco. By the turn of the century sleeping and restaurant cars were operating between all the capitals and most of the principal cities of Europe, North Africa and the Near East.

Working over different systems and crossing frontiers is something of an operating nightmare. There were problems of running, loading gauges, safety regulations, heating, lighting, cooking, refrigeration, not to mention those of customs and currency regulations. As an engineer Nagelmackers understood, was able to foresee and overcome most operating and technical difficulties by making cars and trains as self contained as possible. From the outset it was Wagons-Lits policy to head each of its national divisions or *directions*, as they are known, by an engineer. In Russia there were climatic problems of intense cold, whereas in Egypt and North Africa that of heat. Some trains carried dynamo cars (shades of the Pullman 'pups' – the six-wheel generator vans which were built for the new 1888 all-Pullman train for the London-Brighton service) to provide electricity, others were equipped with gas storage cylinders. Cooking was almost universally by hard fuel since coal, like water, both needed by a steam locomotive, could be picked up anywhere. Food was stored on-board in special closets originally in what the CIWL termed *armoires-glacières* and later in cabinets refrigerated by wet ice. This was made in standard size blocks in all the larger depots.

Nagelmackers was a visionary who devised an organisation which stood the test of time. Though registered in Brussels the Company was operated from Paris. This was the result of early associations with the French railways. France became the largest and most important Wagons-Lits division and Paris the site of the *direction générale*. The French government had a financial investment in Wagons-Lits and it became the custom for the minister of transport to have a seat on the Board as the government nominee. Each country where Wagons-Lits operated had a *direction* in the capital city of the country concerned. Each *direction* had, as appropriate, its own works, sub-offices, agencies and other services. Thus in Paris there were two separate headquarters. One was the *direction générale* which controlled the whole Company, the other was the *direction de Paris* which managed the French operations with extensive works at Saint Denis and stores, cellars and a laundry at Saint-Ouen on the outskirts of the city. Georges Nagelmackers died at his home near Paris at the early age of 60. He was worn out by incessant travelling and by the tough work routine he set himself.

The 1914-18 war caused widespread disruption of services including the loss of the many contracts with Czarist Russia. After the Russian revolution the Wagons-Lits cars were taken over by Soviet Railways where they continued to run for many years. The Armistice between the warring countries was signed at Compiègne outside Paris on 11 November 1918 in Wagons-Lits restaurant car No 2419. Between the wars this car stood as an exhibit at *Les Invalides* in Paris. The car was used again by Adolph Hitler who reconstructed the Compiègne scene when he received the French surrender in 1940. The car was later taken to Germany but was destroyed in Berlin during an air raid.

The between wars period can be described as the Dalziel era for it is he who dominated the Company and directed its destinies until his death at the age of 73 in 1927, by which time 2,000 cars were operating on 50 railways in Europe, Africa and Asia. Soon after Lord Dalziel left the scene the clouds of war started to gather over Europe for the third time in 60 years. Once again Wagons-Lits had to cope with lost contracts and altered schedules as Hitler moved into neighbouring countries. Business went on however and during the brief period of peace between the world wars the Flèche d'Or, the Calais-Paris link of the Golden Arrow was introduced along with the Night Ferry, the Train Bleu and in the Far East the Trans-Manchurian with connections to Peking and Shanghai.

The declaration of war on 3 September 1939 caused widespread dislocation of services and after some semblance of order during the phoney war came the fall of France. In German occupied territories the staff stood by their cars and remained loyal to the Company. In occupied France some were sent to labour camps, others involved in the resistance movement were arrested and imprisoned. Seven were shot by their captors. Thus the second world war represented a very curious period in the annals of Wagons-Lits. Through wise commissariat, supplies were never short. During the time known as the 'occupation' special trains were put at the disposal of members of the Vichy government in unoccupied France, for the German rulers in occupied France and then for the Allied commanders during the liberation of France. During the war itself trains ran whenever and wherever they could; when they did the CIWL restaurant cars, in particular, were well patronised. Though international in outlook the Wagons-Lits is essentially Company minded. Loyalty and dedication to *La Compagnie* comes first and foremost before anything else. This esprit-de-corps runs throughout and explains how quickly the Company always recovers from adversity, and how, despite the loss of some 400 cars, a fleet of 1800 cars was at work in 35 different countries within the span of a few post-war years.

Forty years on from the founder's death in 1905 the organisation of his creation stood up to its most gruelling tests. The pre and post second world war period saw a wholesale nationalisation of railways in Europe, where they were not already state owned. Wagons-Lits was an international company, registered in Brussels and administered in Paris, and could not be nationalised. Each *direction* was self contained and capable, if need be, of operating independently. Even in wartime it was business as usual to an extent and expansions occurred in countries outside the hostile zones. Thus during the second world war there were developments in Spain, Portugal, and particularly in Turkey and the Near Orient. In the early days passengers would complain to Nagelmackers about the poor hotel accommodation and indifferent service in the distant cities to which his cars had conveyed them. This contrasted to the comfort and the on-board service provided by Wagons-Lits trains. Nagelmackers promptly formed a subsidiary and acquired a chain of well run hotels in such places as Cairo, Constantinople (Istanbul), Lisbon, Madrid, Menton, Monte-Carlo, Nice and Paris. Some were purchased, others specially built. It was Wagons-Lits' first venture at diversification which was to develop into a considerable activity. Contracts followed on inland waterways and short sea route vessels and station buffets and refreshment rooms.

In common with Thomas Cook & Son, Wagons-Lits had established important interests in Egypt, dating from 1898, where the cars and the service provided were popular and much favoured, but with political instability these interests lapsed and services were run down during the 1950s; by 1963 most were discontinued, yet in 1981 Wagons-Lits was approached by the Egyptian State Railways to reintroduce a 10-car overnight sleeper between Cairo and Luxor-Aswan.

The Golden Arrow and the Night Ferry were reinstated soon after the second world war as well as most of the famous services on mainland Europe, but by the 1960s times were changing rapidly. Railways the world over were faced by their two by now relentless competitors – the airways and the motorways. Steam had had its day, the great iron horse was being replaced by diesel and by electric traction. The introduction on main lines of high speed, air-conditioned, diesel-electric TEE (Trans-Europ Express) trains, many staffed by CIWL, opened up new doors as others closed.

Today with that ever prevailing efficient management the Compagnie Internationale des Wagons-Lits et du Tourisme, and is subsidiaries, operates hotels, motels, airport and in-flight catering as well as its travel agencies and rail interests of on-train and station catering. In recent times the Company entered a new and profitable field, that of contract catering. Wagons-Lits is also in the preservation market having sold some of its older cars, many built in Britain, to interested parties. One such is the Venice Simplon-Orient-Express Limited subsidiary of Sea Containers Inc, which acquired a variety of Wagons-Lits vehicles for its (London) Boulogne-Paris-Milan-Venice scheduled service, together with a number of Pullman cars for the British section between London Victoria and Folkestone. Of all the many preservation projects the re-creation, by the Sea Co Group, of the Orient Express is the most professional, spectacular, widely publicised and the most heavily financed. The British Pullman cars were beautifully rebuilt and refurbished at Carnforth and the Continental CIWL sleepers, diners, Pullman and staff cars at Bremer Waggonbau at Bremen and Wagons-Lits shops at Ostende. The entire operation was worked out in co-operation with the railways of Britain, France, Italy and Switzerland.

Part of the British section was put on static display at Victoria Station, London on 11 November 1981 formed:

Locomotive: electro-diesel No 73142 *Broadlands*

Cygnus	(P)	*Ibis*	(K)	
Perseus	(P)	*Phoenix*	(P)	Baggage brake No 7*

*Converted from an LNER 1944 built carrier pigeon transporter brake van.
Since then other cars have been added including *Audrey*, one of the Brighton Belle cars.

At the present time the on-train food and beverage role on the railways, particularly with French Railways (SNCF), with whom Wagons-Lits has always been closely associated, has changed to that of a contractor. CIWLT no longer provides the vehicles and operates them. The cars are now SNCF owned and on the majority of lines, CIWLT operated. Wagons-Lits may have been founded in 1876 but well over a century later it is still one of the most efficient and progressive transport catering, travel and tourist organisations in the world.

4 Pullman on the Southern

PULLMAN cars worked on the Southern originally through its constituent, the London, Brighton & South Coast almost without a break from 1875 to 1972. The association was very close, for the Pullman Car Company had its operating offices on the Southern at Victoria Station, and its depot stores on railway premises at Battersea, where they had moved from London Bridge. Preston Park Pullman works were sited in the old LBSCR paint shop from 1928 when they moved from the former LCDR works at Longhedge, by Stewarts Lane. Moreover all the Pullman officers lived on the Southern.

Though the Company also operated at various times on parts of the LNER, LMS and GWR, and their nationalised Eastern, Midland, Scottish and Western region successors, its most concentrated operations were, for almost its entire history, on Southern lines. When, as the Pullman Division, operations on the Southern were phased out in the 1960s and the offices moved from Victoria to Paddington, it was to spell, intentionally or otherwise, the beginning of the end of Pullman as an entity.

Pullman was involved in the various passenger class nomenclature changes since although three class ordinary travel of Victorian years gradually became two class — first and third — three classes survived on Continental boat trains until two classes, called first and second, became standard in Europe and in Britain in June 1956.

The Central Division

Although Pullmans started running on the LBSCR soon after they were introduced to the Midland Railway there has been

41

controversy on which was the first car to work on the Brighton line. The first was the sleeper *Mars* suitably adapted as a parlour. American built and Derby assembled, it went into traffic on 20 October 1875. It was a kind of demonstration car and caused much excitement. After a few years service on the Brighton line the car was sent to Italy. The second car was the famous *Jupiter*, which also spent two years, from 1882 in an LCDR boat train before returning to Brighton. In 1915 it was downclassed, redesignated Car No 1 and put into the Newhaven service. The third notable car sent to Brighton, from the Midland, was the parlour *Globe* in 1878; it was renamed *Beatrice* in 1881 and had the distinction of being the first car to be lit by electricity from batteries recharged at the end of each trip.

As in the USA, from single car workings the next logical step was a train made up entirely of Pullman cars. The first was inaugurated in 1881 consisting of *Maud, Louise, Victoria* and *Beatrice*, and known as the Pullman Limited Express. The term Limited meant that the accommodation was limited to the number of seats, all of which were bookable in advance. Meanwhile while single car workings, started in 1875, loaded well. In 1888 the Pullman Limited Express was replaced by a three-car vestibuled set made up of a parlour *Albert Victor*; a buffet car *Prince* and a smoking car *Princess*. The train was completed with two matching six-wheel railway vans, known as Pullman pups. One of the vans carried a dynamo which provided electric lighting. The service proved popular and was augmented as required. From then on the term express was seldom used on the Brighton line, and a non-stop train was known as a fast.

In 1898 a new Pullman service was introduced known as the Brighton Limited, a five car train of *Victoria, Beatrice, Princess of Wales, Duchess of York* and *Her Majesty* which ran on Sundays only. In 1908 the Pullman car had become so popular it was decided to run a seven-car train seven days a week all year round. It went into traffic on 8 November and was called the Southern Belle. The original make-up was *Verona* and *Alberta*, parlour brakes; *Grosvenor*, buffet car; and parlours *Cleopatra*,

THE PULLMAN CAR COMPANY LIMITED.

21st Anniversary "Southern Belle"

November 1st, 1929

Luncheon 4s. 6d.

□

MENU

HORS D'ŒUVRE CHOISIS

CONSOMMÉ ROYALE

□

TURBOT POCHÉ   SAUCE HOLLANDAISE

□

CANARD RÔTI

CÔTELETTES D'AGNEAU REFORME

LEGUMES

BUFFET FROID

□

POUDING PRINCESSE

MACÉDOINE DE FRUITS AUX LIQUEURS

□

FROMAGE   CÉLERI   BISCUITS

□

CAFÉ

Example of a pre-second world war menu. The Southern Belle anniversary was pre-electrification.

Belgravia, Bessborough and *Princess Helen*, with suitable cars as spares. The Southern Belle was steam hauled until the line was electrified by the Southern; on 1 January 1933 it was replaced by a brand new electric Pullman train which a year later was renamed the Brighton Belle to avoid confusion with the newly-introduced Bournemouth Belle.

The Brighton Belle

The Brighton Belle was one of the best known trains in the world. It was also the first all-Pullman electric train, since the motor coaches were parlour brakes. Though there were several other Pullman Belles, the Brighton was always known as *the* Belle. Three five-car units were built for the service, each formed with two first class kitchen cars and three third class cars – one parlour and two motor parlour brakes. Following the custom the firsts were named, and the thirds numbered. The thirds had two + two seating in contrast to two + one in locomotive-hauled stock.

Brighton Belle Units, SR Class 5BEL					
Unit Nos	3051	3052	3053	*Seats*	
Cars				1st	3rd
Motor Third Parlour Brake	88	90	92		48
First Kitchen	*Hazel*	*Audrey*	*Gwen*	20	
First Kitchen	*Doris*	*Vera*	*Mona*	20	
Third Parlour	86	87	85		56
Motor Third Parlour Brake	89	91	93		48
				40	152

For most of its life the Brighton Belle service was London based with a six-trip Monday–Saturday schedule and four on Sundays. Towards the end the service became Brighton-based with two more Monday–Saturday trips added, making eight in all. When London-based the 5BEL units in traffic were stabled either at Battersea Pier or in the Dip, Victoria Station. When Brighton based the units were stabled at Lovers Walk sidings just outside Brighton station. According to the bookings the Belle ran as a

THE BRIGHTON BELLE

Bill of Fare

SNACK SERVICE

Soup of the day with Golden Croutons		1/6
Deep Fried Fillet of Fish Tartare with French Fried Potatoes		8/6
Pan Fried Egg and Grilled Bacon (Single) 4/–	Double	8/–
Welsh Rarebit 2/9 Buck Rarebit		4/–
Grilled Sirloin Steak with Tomato,		
French Fried Potatoes and Garden Peas		12/6
Sausages (each) 1/2 Bacon (portion)		2/9
Tomatoes on Toast		2/9
Eggs divers styles (each)		1/4
A Pair of Grilled Kippers		3/6
Grilled Chipolata Sausages and Whipped Potatoes		3/6
Cold Collation and Mixed Dressed Salad		8/6

BEVERAGES

Tea	per pot, per person	1/6
Coffee	per pot, per person	2/–
Milk	per glass	1/3
Bovril	per pot, per person	1/8

SANDWICHES (full round)

Assorted Centres (Plain)	2/6
Toasted Bacon Sandwich with pickles	4/–
Double Decker Egg and Bacon Sandwich	5/6

SUNDRIES

Cut Hovis and White Bread and Butter (two rounds)		8d.
Buttered Toast (per round)		9d.
Roll and Curled Butter		9d.
Cheeses: (Portion) English Farmhouse 1/3	Continental	1/6
Quality Cake		9d.
Biscuits Sweet (Packet)		6d.
Biscuits Cheese Dry		3d.
Individual Preserves, Jam, Honey, Marmalade		6d.

PLEASE ASK FOR A BILL AND RETAIN IT

In case of difficulty will passengers please see the *Conductor*
or write to
*General Manager, British Rail Catering,
14 Bishop's Bridge Road, London, W.2*
enclosing your bill.

The all day bill-of-fare on the Brighton Belle 1966, before the kippers came off but after the BR double arrow logo replaced the Pullman coat-of-arms.

single or a double unit, and there was no fixed working. The third unit was held as a spare at Steatham Hill or Lovers Walk. How they were staffed is described in chapter 11.

Traditionally Victoria to Brighton was a 60 minute non-stop run, but later with improved track and signalling the timing was reduced to 55 and 56 minutes though the Belle was unable latterly to maintain this fast running in comfort and was kept on the 60 minute schedule. Departure times remained fairly constant but there were changes in later years. This is the eight-trip Monday–Saturday roster in 1963/4:

BRIGHTON BELLE TIMINGS

Brighton	09.40*	* Retimed 09.25
Victoria	11.00	June 1966
Brighton	13.25	
Victoria	15.00	
Brighton	17.25	
Victoria	19.00	
Brighton	20.25	
Victoria	23.00	

At Victoria from 1963 onwards the Belle used platform 17 where an archway was installed at the barrier end. In its final years the traditional Belle timings were altered to conform with new timetables on the Central Division.

Over the years the Belle was very popular with theatricals living in Brighton. The 1963 retiming was particularly welcomed since it enabled the regulars to commute on the first up and the last down trip. A Belle regular, or should it be irregular, was the Southern's Chief Mechanical Engineer the great Oliver Bulleid. He was known to Pullman as an individualist, something of an autocrat and an eccentric who would get his office to reserve a seat on the 19.00 Belle and then not travel, having presumably missed his train – a crime in itself for any railman let alone a CME! It meant that the train left a passenger light when the seat, first class at that, might have been filled by a fare paying passenger, so Pullman lost a supplement.

For a short period after the second world war until 1957, a unit was used for the Sunday only Eastbourne Pullman, sometimes erroneously (and unofficially) referred to as the Eastbourne Belle which left Victoria at 10.40 taking 1 hour 20 minutes. It returned from Eastbourne at 17.45.

In 1967 Pullman management passed to British Rail Catering (later Travellers-Fare) from the Pullman Division; the Brighton Belle then had five more years to run. The three units were refurbished, the running names and numbers of the cars removed, they reverted and were known by their schedule numbers, and the sets were repainted in the BR standard blue and grey livery. The name Brighton Belle was painted on the waist panels with the BR double arrow logo replacing the Pullman coat-of-arms. The uniforms of the staff were also changed.

When the end of the Belle was announced the protests were many. But when sometime in 1969 one of the train's regular commuters, Lord Olivier, the actor-manager, found one morning he could no longer obtain his usual pair of 'marvellous, juicy and succulent' grilled kippers for breakfast, it became a *cause célèbre*. A petition was organised, Lord Olivier was interviewed and the national press naturally got hold of the story. Apparently an over zealous official had streamlined the breakfast menu for *economic reasons*. So great was the hue and cry the kippers were promptly reinstated on the breakfast menu. But when the announcement came that the Belle was definitely coming off and that it would not be replaced the news was hailed as a disaster of the first magnitude. But off it came on Sunday 30 April 1972. The Belle died in a blaze of glory.

The Belle sets were often used for charter specials and occasionally for Royal journeys. On 26 March 1948, unit 3053, *Gwen* and *Mona*, (the units were usually known by the names of the first class cars) conveyed Queen Elizabeth (later The Queen Mother) from Victoria to Brighton and return. Both journeys were on regular fast timings. The outward trip was on the 14.00 down from Victoria when the 5BEL was attached to the regular six coach 6PUL set (see later). The return was on the 17.25 up

Belle timing when 3053 was attached to the booked 5BEL unit.

The next important 5BEL specials were in connection with the Coronation Review of the Fleet at Spithead in 1953. Unit 3052 *Audrey* and *Vera* was selected for three special trips. On Monday 15 June it conveyed the Queen Mother, Princess Margaret and other members of the Royal Family from Waterloo at 12.50 to Portsmouth arriving at 14.35. Luncheon was served en-route. *Audrey* was the Royal car on all trips.

The Queen Mother returned to Windsor in the 5BEL the same day leaving Portsmouth Harbour at 18.30 and arriving at Windsor & Eton Riverside at 20.05. The unit then ran empty from Riverside at 20.35 to Fratton Carriage Shed, arriving at 22.20 to be made ready to form the 09.35 from Portsmouth Harbour on Tuesday 16 June to convey the Queen and the Duke of Edinburgh to Windsor. The unit then left empty at 11.48 for Wimbledon Park Depot arriving 12.55 to make its way back to Streatham Hill to stand spare until required for traffic, its Royal duty over for that year.

The following year on 14 April 1954, 3052 was booked for a Royal train to convey the Queen Mother, Princess Margaret, Prince Charles and Princess Anne from Waterloo to Portsmouth Harbour. It was the first time the future Prince of Wales had travelled in, or had seen, an electric train at close quarters and enquired of S. W. Smart, the Superintendent of Operation, if there was a man in front. On the trip down Prince Charles and Princess Anne were taken through the train by S. W. Smart and F. D. M. Harding into the driver's cab to meet the motorman.

3052 was again used as a Royal on 13 November 1964 to convey the Queen from Victoria to Brighton. It was attached to the regular 5BEL leaving at 11.00. No 3052 was reserved for the exclusive use of the Royal party and accompanying railway officers; the Queen herself travelled in *Audrey*. As the bookings were heavy the third 5BEL was brought into service and ran as a relief to the 11.00. It was always a rare sight to see all three Belle units in traffic either at Victoria or at Brighton station at the same time. An unusual working involving all three units occurred on Tuesday 2 June 1953, Coronation Day. A party of

300 staying at the Metropole Hotel, Brighton were booked on the Belle from Brighton to Victoria and return to see the Coronation. It had to be an early departure with breakfast served on the forward journey, and afternoon tea on the return. To accommodate the Gordon Hotels party — the Metropole, Brighton was still part of the Gordon Hotel chain — two 5BEL units were booked. Bearing in mind that in 1953 the Brighton Belle was a London based service, on 2 June 1953 it was retimed as follows:

05.05	Brighton to Victoria (Gordon Hotel party)
11.00	Victoria to Brighton
13.25	Brighton to Victoria
15.00	Victoria to Brighton
17.25	Brighton to Victoria
19.05	Victoria to Brighton (Gordon Hotel party)
20.25	Brighton to Victoria

The third 5BEL ran empty from Streatham Hill to form the regular 19.00 Victoria to Brighton working. The unit then shunted to Lovers Walk. To serve 150 breakfasts from the two kitchens in each unit in 60 minutes took some doing; afternoon tea was less hectic.

The Machine Tool Trades Association Special on 3 July 1956 was a spectacular affair, and its promoter Major Cyril Dennis an ebullient showman. Two units of the *Brighton Belle* were hired to take a party of 300 from Victoria to Hove and return. A five course dinner was served on the forward journey and a full English breakfast on the return in the early hours. The ten car train ran in the following times:

Victoria	dep 20.42	Hove	dep 01.45
Hove	arr 21.57	Victoria	arr 03.05

On arrival at Hove a fleet of coaches took the party along the seafront to a gala ball at the Royal Pavillion, Brighton.

The Major, a stickler for detail, thought of everything. He

devised the menus, selected the wines, specified where they should be purchased and even chose the programme of music the Southern Railway Band would play as the guests boarded the train at platform 17. A coupé was reserved in one of the first class cars, equipped as a first aid post with a doctor and two nurses in attendance should any of the party be taken ill. When the Major entertained and put on a show there were no half measures.

If Major Dennis's big show was spectacular the Regency Belle, under direction of Lionel Burleigh, was a colourful affair. The charter consisted of hiring a 5BEL unit to convey parties of guests to Brighton starting on Saturday 28 and Sunday 29 March 1964 and running on each consecutive weekend thereafter. It ran to the following schedule:

Victoria	dep 19.17	Brighton	dep 02.15
Brighton	arr 20.25	Victoria	arr 03.30

The promotor decorated the train with floral displays and the Pullman crew was augmented by a bevy of glamorous young ladies in Regency dress who acted as hostesses; but let the publicity hand-out (see page 53) tell the story.

The project attracted widespread publicity and on 28 March the Regency Belle got off to a flying start. On the first weekend a 5BEL was booked on both nights, but thereafter, on account of essential civil engineering work, a diversion had to be made via Steyning over non-electrified lines. This necessitated forming a locomotive-hauled Pullman train to run just on the Saturday night until the civil engineering work was completed. The locomotive-hauled train was stabled at Stewarts Lane and formed as follows:

A	Car No 64	42 seats
B	*Evadne*	20 seats
C	*Octavia*	20 seats
D	*Lydia*	20 seats
E	*Phyllis*	20 seats
F	Car No 334	30 seats
G	Car No 84	42 seats
	Total	194 seats

The locomotive was usually Bulleid Battle of Britain No 34088 *213 Squadron*.

Observation car *Maid of Morven* built in 1914, coupled to a rake of four
Pullman cars for Caledonian service.

The Torquay Pullman standing at platform 4 at Paddington in 1929.

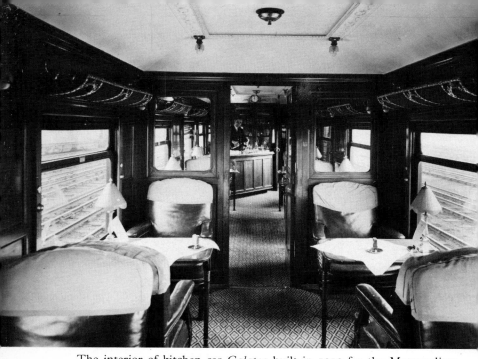

The interior of kitchen car *Galatea* built in 1910 for the Metropolitan Railway. Note the glass-fronted cabinet behind the attendant for the display of spirits in miniature bottles and for tobacco goods. (*London Transport*)

Shipping Pullman cars to Ireland in 1926.

The Regency Belle

IF you would like to get away from it all for a few hours and enjoy a really carefree night out in good company, reserve a seat on 'The Regency Belle'. Leave your ignition key at home. Go to Victoria Station on Saturday or Sunday night at 7.00 for 7.15 departure. Pass under the gay awning, along the red carpet to the 'Regency Belle', the most luxurious train in the world staffed by efficient stewards and six of Britain's most beautiful girls in immaculate Regency costume, who will escort you to your reserved seat in an atmosphere of soft lighting and very quiet Gershwin music. There will be an orchid for every lady, and on the journey down you sip your vintage champagne and relax. Our charming hostesses will be glad to talk and give advice or help to visitors, on where to dine, dance or play in this Country, and other points of interest.

They are conversant with the Ballet, the Theatre and the Arts, and have been specially chosen for their knowledge and ability to put people completely at ease. In fact, if this is your first visit to these shores, you will get a wonderful insight into our way of life, or at least one facet of it. Why not make this your initial foray!

Upon arrival you will be given a 'V.I.P.' welcome by one of Brighton's celebrated personalities of whom there are many. A fleet of luxurious cars will then drive you to a first class hotel where you will partake of a recherché supper in delightful surroundings. After this, dancing; a midnight swim? or a mild flutter at the gaming tables and then—idle chatter until your carriage arrives at 1.45 to transport you back to your softly heated luxury train.

Then the perfect English breakfast will be served as only this Country knows how to cook it. Finnon Haddock, crisp Wiltshire bacon, Sussex eggs, buttered toast and chunky marmalade with tea or coffee. All this and the morning papers too!

A night to remember and the cost £7 7s. od.

Interested?

Tickets may be obtained at the General Enquiry Office at Victoria Station, the British Railway Travel Centre, Lower Regent Street, London, W.1, or you may write to the Line Manager, B.R., Essex House, College Road, Croydon, Surrey.

Direction of Lionel Burleigh

Printed by FERMAPRINT, London & New York.

When this train was used the return arrival was retimed to 04.01. Normally the 5BEL empties were from Streatham Hill, but when the locomotive-hauled train was used, the 5BEL for the Sunday worked up from Lovers Walk. After working the special on the Sunday night the unit ran to Streatham Hill to take up the 11.00 Victoria Belle scheduled on the Monday morning. The train ran for several weekends but the Sunday run was soon cancelled. The Regency Belle last ran on Saturday 18 April as the Saturday April 25 run was cancelled on the Friday afternoon, regrettably through lack of support.

More stories could be told of the Belle than of any other Pullman train. But like all trains it was the scene on-board of adventure and romance and also on occasions of sorrow and even tragedy. On Friday 14 October 1960 after the 15.00 down and before the 17.25 up when the train shunted to Lovers Walk, the body of a young girl, a student, was found in a lavatory of car 86 of unit 3051. She had committed suicide, a broken love affair, it was said.

Other Brighton Line Pullmans
Apart from the Belle, Pullman cars ran as single or double car workings, on other parts of the LBSCR and the Central Division of the Southern. There was the City Limited which started in 1907, a predominantly first class train which ran from Brighton to London Bridge and return on business timings. Cars also ran to Eastbourne and Hastings and to Littlehampton via Hove and West Worthing. Cars ran in the Newhaven boat train from Victoria.

The SR's 1930s Brighton line electrification was in two phases; on 1 January 1933 the lines from Victoria and London Bridge to Brighton, Worthing (and later to Littlehampton) were completed and on 7 July 1935 to Ore via Eastbourne, Bexhill and Hastings. The change from steam to electric traction brought new ideas and practices to the Pullman Car Company. It also meant 38 new vehicles, 15 as we have seen for the Belle service and the balance of 23 for the single car workings which extended in a great triangle from London to Ore and

Littlehampton. The latter were the composite cars with 12 first class (including a coupé for four), and 16 third class seats, and including kitchen, pantry, and lavatory. All the new Pullmans were built by Metropolitan Cammell although several contractors were involved with interior furnishings in order to obtain variety in decor. Cooking was by electricity, the supply being taken off the third rail by the motor coaches and carried to the Pullman cars by a jumper cable through the coaches. Each of the 23 composite cars was marshalled with five railway vehicles with first and third class accommodation, into a six-car unit known as a 6PUL, and formed: motor saloon brake third, trailer third, trailer composite, Pullman car (KL), trailer composite, motor saloon brake third. Three of the units though were classified originally as 6CIT and were intended to cover the City Limited timings of 08.45 Brighton to London Bridge and 17.00 London Bridge to Brighton. The 6CIT units as built for the replacement steam service had a predominance of first class accommodation — three first class trailers instead of composites and a third. After the second world war when full service was resumed the 6CIT sets were altered to conform with the first and third seating of the rest of the 6PUL units. Even so in the ways of railwaymen, the altered units were always referred to as City stock and the timings, especially the 17.00 from London Bridge as the City Limited. With the Brighton Belle, the Central Division composite Pullman cars provided one of the most concentrated Pullman services in the world. They operated almost round the clock on complex working sheets, a railway operating phenomenon of which the Southern was a pastmaster on its electric services.

In addition to the 6PUL units the SR built 17 six-car corridor units known as 6PAN sets. The PAN classification derived from the pantry, a kind of mini-buffet, built into a section of a 30 seat first class vehicle, to provide a service of light refreshments. In these units the pantry vehicle took the place of a Pullman car but was staffed by Pullman under contract. As catering vehicles they were most unsatisfactory, badly designed, inadequate and without cooking equipment. They were intended for a corridor service along the train, always a precarious affair especially when the train was crowded and the corridor blocked by passengers. A limited service could be provided to passengers at the flap in the door of the pantry but it was not very convenient. Plans were discussed to convert the pantry cars into half-buffets, an ideal solution, but the modifications did not get beyond the talking stage. Pullman was lumbered with the PAN units; in time staffing was reduced from two attendants to one but eventually the pantries were closed. These unusual vehicles were sometimes known as the Eastbourne pantry cars, since they were originally intended for services to that town. The units usually worked as doubles, one 6PUL coupled to a 6PAN, but there was no corridor access between the two units.

At the outbreak of war on 3 September 1939 all catering vehicles were either withdrawn or locked up. Four months later on 1 January 1940 a few Pullmans were reinstated, the windows blacked out and the cars camouflaged, but on 22 May 1942 all cars were finally taken out of service and stored for the duration of hostilities on lonely sidings. On the night of 9/10 October 1940 Belle unit 3052 standing at platform 17 at Victoria was badly damaged in an air raid. The final count after the war was four Pullman cars from all services destroyed and 120 damaged by enemy action.

The Southern Electric Pullman cars gradually returned to service from May 1946. The Brighton Belle service was partially reinstated on 12 October 1946 but as a 5BEL + 6PUL formation since 3052 had not yet been repaired. Only 3051 and 3053 were available for traffic. On 6 October 1947, a year later, the Belle service was fully restored with two units for traffic and one spare, just in time for the winter timetable.

The 23 composite cars rated among the most famous class of all Pullman vehicles. The cars were named and a record of these names must go down in Pullman history. It is more the pity only two out of the 23 are known to have been preserved, *Bertha* and *Ruth*. At the end of their long and busy lives the 6PUL units were phased out of traffic commencing September 1965 and completed by June 1966. During the changeover period there were considerable formation changes on SR electric units which also involved the Pullman cars until the old stock was finally withdrawn. The 6PUL/PAN units were replaced by new rolling stock, including buffet facilities built into one half of a second class coach and suitable for single manning. The trains were formed as four-car units classified 4CIG and 4BIG, the latter including the buffet car. The IG part of the classification came from the old telegraphic code letters for Brighton. The 4BIG buffets came under the management of British Rail Catering.

The 23 Brighton Composite Pullman Cars

Pre-War Unit Nos	Name	Post-War Unit Nos
3001	*Anne*	3012*
3002	*Rita*	3043*
3003	*Grace*	3003
3004	*Elinor*	3004
3005	*Ida*	3005
3006	*Rose*	3006
3007	*Violet*	3007
3008	*Lorna*	3008
3009	*Alice*	3009
3010	*Daisy*	3010
3011	*Naomi*	3011
3012	*Bertha*	3001*
3013	*Brenda*	3013
3014	*Enid*	3014
3015	*Joyce*	3015
3016	*Iris*	3016
3017	*Ruth*	3042*
3018	*May*	3041*
3019	*Peggy*	3019
3020	*Clara*	3020
3041	*Gwladys*	3017*
3042	*Olive*	3002*
3043	*Ethel*	3018*

*Unit change

1932 Original Unit Numbers
2001–2020   6PUL
2041–2043   6CIT

1936 Unit Numbers Change
3001–3020   6PUL
3041–3043   6CIT

1946
6CIT units became part of 6PUL stock.

Occasionally 6PUL units were used for Royal specials. Earlier in this chapter it was noted that for the Spithead Review on 15 June 1953 a 5BEL unit took the Queen Mother and other members of the Royal Family to Portsmouth Harbour. The Queen Mother returned in 3052 from Portsmouth Harbour to Windsor & Eton Riverside. Princess Margaret and the other members of the royal party left Portsmouth Harbour at 23.35 also for Windsor & Eton Riverside, arriving at 01.32 on the 16 June, and travelling in *Peggy* of 6PUL unit 3019.

Three previous occasions are recorded when a 6PUL was used for a royal special. On 14 July 1948 Princess Margaret travelled in car *Ethel* of unit 3018, working the 11.45 from Victoria, to Glynde, where a special stop was made for Glyndebourne. The service came up from Ore as a double 6PUL to make the 11.45 down so that a Pullman car was available for other passengers. On 22 July 1955 the Queen Mother travelled in *Naomi* of unit 3011 on the 18.25 Brighton to Victoria, and the same car was used for Princess Margaret on 26 October 1955 on the 13.00 Victoria to Brighton returning on the 16.25 Brighton to Victoria.

During LBSCR days and while steam services survived on the SR, Pullman cars ran from Victoria and London Bridge to Arundel, Chichester, Bognor and Portsmouth via the mid-Sussex line through Horsham. When the line was electrified on 3 July 1938, the Pullman cars were replaced by 13 buffet cars marshalled into four-car corridor electric units classified as 4BUF sets which were usually coupled to one or two 4COR units without buffets. The Bognor buffets, as they were called, were based at Bognor and did not normally run through to Portsmouth. The cars were exceedingly well designed with a buffet counter, saloon with tables and seating, and a very well equipped kitchen. The Bognor buffets represented some of the best railway-built catering vehicles. Even now, over 40 years later, they would be considered contemporary and serviceable.

The policy with railway owned vehicles – 'ROV' – on the Southern needs explanation. Until 1963, if Pullman supplement cars were replaced by ROVs following a major operating change with electrification or dieselisation, the replacement railway-owned catering vehicles were staffed and operated by the Pullman Car Company. There was an operating difference between an ROV and a Pullman car since the ROV cars were wholly maintained by the railway, which collected from the Pullman Car Company a five per cent subvention on takings. As this subvention was on *takings* and not *profits* the arrangement was satisfactory to the railway, if not always to the contractor. It must be emphasised that the ROVs were in no way inferior in catering standards to a Pullman supplement car, for the Pullman Car Company had a reputation to maintain. Both before and after the second world war, Pullman operated a variety of ROVs on the Southern, including locomotive-hauled restaurant and buffet cars on Eastern and Central Divisions. Not all ROVs on the Southern, though, were Pullman operated. A fleet of ROVs worked on the Western Division out of Waterloo and on a number of cross country services, which were operated by Spiers & Pond, then later Frederick Hotels (who paid a seven per cent subvention on sales) before they were taken over after 1948 by BTC's Hotels Executive.

Pullman cars worked the Newhaven-Dieppe boat trains as early as 1891. After the second world war the veteran buffets *Grosvenor*, with *Myrtle* as the standby vehicle, were allocated to the Newhaven service until replaced by ROV buffets. Though the line to the harbour was electrified in 1947 the boat trains continued to be steam hauled until 1949 when electric locomotives took over. In due course the locomotive-hauled trains were replaced by electric multiple-unit stock with buffet cars. Pullman cars also ran in charter and race trains to Epsom, Lingfield, Plumpton and Gatwick – the latter before the great airport was built.

In 1949 the Southern and London Midland regions reinstated a version of the pre-war Sunny South Express which ran at weekends, during the summer, between Hastings, Coventry and Birmingham via Eastbourne, Brighton, Redhill and the West London line. Pullman staffed and operated a railway-owned restaurant car in the Southern Region train based at Hastings and thus worked on to the LMR, but as far as Pullman was concerned the Company was only involved in this working for a year or two although the train itself and variations continued – and indeed as part of BR's cross country Inter-City network survives today between Brighton and Manchester. A little publicised Pullman service in 1908 connected Uckfield with London Bridge and Victoria via Crowborough, Eridge, Edenbridge Town, Oxted and East Croydon. It was advertised as a breakfast car in the morning and a teatime car in the evening.

The South Eastern Division

In many respects the biggest and most sustained activity on the former South Eastern & Chatham section of the Southern was the boat train traffic in its heyday, sadly now a bygone age. The Pullman boat train story commenced on 1 July 1882 when the stalwart *Jupiter* was loaned to the LCDR from the LBSCR to run in a boat service which left Victoria at 10.00 and returned from Dover Pier at 15.30. It was known as the Dover Pullman Car Boat Train Express. The service was just moderately successful but came off on 31 July 1884. Pullman did not return to the boat trains until 1910. In between, during the period from 1889 to 1893 the two rival companies – the South Eastern, and the London, Chatham & Dover, introduced Continental Club Trains, both trains being supplied and staffed by Wagons-Lits and running as boat train services between London and Dover. Thereby hangs a tale of the personal rivalry of two powerful and influential figures, Sir Edward William Watkin, MP (1819–1901) chairman of the SER, and James Staats Forbes (1823–1904) chairman of the LCDR. Each tried to ruin the other, without succeeding, age and illness eventually settling the issue.

James Staats Forbes was general manager of the LCDR before becoming its chairman. He was also chairman of the District Railway in London. Forbes stole a march on his rival by introducing a Club Train. Sir Edward Watkin, originally general manager and then chairman of the Manchester, Sheffield & Lincolnshire Railway – later the Great Central –

was also chairman of the Metropolitan Railway, and the East London Railway as well as the SER. Through his Metropolitan interests he already had a series of clashes with Forbes over the District Railway. Sir Edward planned, as part of his Continental link, to develop a great London terminus at Baker Street, or at Moorgate, on the Metropolitan, which he regarded as a main line railway. How dare Forbes put on a Club Train! Immediately Sir Edward contacted Wagons-Lits for a similar train for his SER, and Georges Nagelmackers was only too happy to oblige. Each three or four car Club Train of parlour and kitchen cars, specially built to conform to British loading gauge, left London at the same time, 16.15, the SER train from Charing Cross, the LCDR from Victoria. The former was scheduled to arrive at Dover Pier at 17.55, the latter at 18.00. The locals took bets as to which train would arrive first. There was a similar race against time on the return to London. But the fast and reckless running was no more appreciated than the Watkin-Forbes rivalry, and the Club Trains cost the two railways dearly before being taken off; 43 years were to pass before Wagons-Lits vehicles returned to Britain with the 1936 inauguration of the Night Ferry.

Sir Edward Watkin was no lover of Pullman; it is possible he nursed a similar dislike of George Pullman, Davison Dalziel, or both, as he did of Forbes. One wonders what Sir Edward would have said when nine years after his death two Pullmans *Mayflower* and *Galatea*, were introduced on his favourite railway, the Metropolitan, on 1 June 1910. The cars ran on services between Aylesbury and Chesham to Liverpool Street and Aldgate via Baker Street. They proved popular with City businessmen; with a supplement of 6d ($2\frac{1}{2}$p) or later 1s (5p) on top of the first class fare they could hardly fail. They ran through the day and on late theatre trains when supper was served. One of the cars was in a special train on 9 December 1932 for the opening ceremony of the Stanmore branch. Apart from the first world war years *Mayflower* and *Galatea* ran until 7 October 1939. They were not reintroduced or replaced after the second war and ended their days as offices of a merchant at Hinchley Wood on the Southern before they were broken up.

The Metropolitan Pullmans started a relationship between Pullman and what was to become London Transport, for Lord Ashfield of Southwell (the creator of London Transport) followed Lord Dalziel as chairman of Pullman in 1927; 30 years on another head of London Transport, Sir John Elliot, became chairman of the Pullman Company. LTE had an efficient industrial catering set-up complete with excellent training facilities. Pullman was then able, through Sir John, to take advantage of them and a series of refresher courses were arranged for Pullman car chefs at the LTE headquarters, 55 Broadway, above St James station on the Circle Line. London Transport always maintained a good standard of catering throughout the whole of its organisation and in later years the standards maintained in the 55 Broadway messes came in for some unfair criticism for being too high!

Pullmans returned to South Eastern boat traffic on 21 March 1910, between Charing Cross and Dover and between Victoria and Folkestone on the by then singly managed SECR. Six cars were built for these services, kitchen cars *Clementina*, *Florence* and *Valencia*, and parlour cars *Corunna*, *Savona* and *Sorrento*, converted later to kitchens.

The Golden Arrow

Long before the devastating impact of air travel and car ferries, the between-the-wars period was the golden age of Continental boat train traffic. The Folkestone-Boulogne, Dover-Calais, and Dover-Ostend services would run in multi-portions, each train with Pullman cars and frequently in numerous round trips. Conductor George Hubbard of Hastings recalled when, as a boy new on the Company, he received a duty to work the Ostend. On arriving at Victoria he discovered the service was running in seven portions! On 25 May 1929 a new Continental service, the Golden Arrow was inaugurated by Sir Herbert Walker, the creator of the Southern Railway. If the Brighton Belle was the best known, the Golden Arrow was the most famous of all Pullman trains and certainly the most exclusive. Its counterpart across the Channel was a train of CIWL Pullman cars, the Flèche d'Or.

GOLDEN ARROW

FLÈCHE D'OR

a la Carte

SANDWICHES

Smoked Salmon	Chicken	(Full Round)	3/6
Ham and other Centres			2/6

AFTERNOON TEA 4/–

Toasted Tea Cake   Hot Buttered Toast
Fruit Loaf, White and Hovis Bread and Butter
Teatime Biscuits   Individual Preserves   Quality Cake
Pot of Tea (Indian or China)

SUNDRIES

Cut Hovis and White Bread and Butter	1/–
Toast and Curled Butter	1/–
Toasted Teacake	1/–
Fruit Cake	1/–
Biscuits	1/–
Preserves, Jam, Honey	1/–

A LA CARTE DISHES Featured on the Inward Service

Smoked Salmon with Lemon Wedges	9/6
Omelette to Choice	7/6
Pan Fried Egg and Grilled Bacon (single) 3/3 (double)	6/6
Grilled Dover Sole with French Fried Potatoes	10/6

BEVERAGES

Indian Tea, China Tea, Russian Tea, per pot per person	1/6
Coffee per cup 1/– per pot per person	2/–

The TRIANON BAR in this train

offers a pleasant meeting place.

CIGARETTES

Rothman's King Size   Player's Medium   Player's Gold Leaf
Bristol   Senior Service   Piccadilly No. 1.
Havana Cigars : Partagas Cubanos 5/6 Punch Petit Coronation 7/–
Manikin Cigars (packet of 5) 4/–

Swan Vestas 5d.   Aspro 7d.

PLEASE ASK FOR A BILL AND RETAIN IT

The tariff on the Golden Arrow 1963 before the Trianon Bar was withdrawn.

The Golden Arrow made a daily round trip from Victoria to Dover where it awaited the incoming passengers from Paris for the return run to London. The Pullman Car Company conductors originally travelled through to Paris, returning with their passengers the following day. After the second world war the conductor travelled only as far as Calais, a daily instead of a two day trip, but even so they travelled some 50,000 miles a year and in all weathers. Mal de mer on a rough Channel crossing was one of the hazards of the job. The Golden Arrow conductors were personalities, the best known being Walter Badger, who, before retiring after 50 years' service, was promoted to chief inspector, the only Pullman official to hold that rank.

The traditional departure timings from No 8 platform at Victoria were 10.00 in winter and 11.00 in British summertime. The timings varied though and in order to meet the Wagons-Lits requirement of running one instead of two trains between Calais Maritime and Paris Nord the Golden Arrow ran for a time in the mid 1960s to Folkestone Harbour on the outward service on an early afternoon timing and then ran empty to Dover Marine for the up trip.

GOLDEN ARROW – SUMMER – 1962

London, Victoria	dep 11.00	Paris, Nord	dep 12.39
Dover Marine	arr 12.22	Calais Maritime	arr 15.45
	dep 12.50		dep 16.10
Calais Maritime	arr 14.10	Dover Marine	arr 17.30
	dep 14.40		dep 18.10
Paris, Nord	arr 17.50	London, Victoria	arr 19.35

From its inception until 1939 the Arrow was hauled by a Maunsell King Arthur or a Lord Nelson 4–6–0. The reinstated train in 1946 was initially worked by a new class of engine, Bulleid's Merchant Navy 4–6–2, the first being 21C1 (BR 35001) *Channel Packet*.

Later the lighter Bulleid Pacifics, the West Country and Battle of Britain types took over from the Merchant Navies, but from 1951 the Arrow was also worked by a BR Britannia 4–6–2 including No 70004 *William Shakespeare* and No 70014 *Iron Duke*. The final steam working was on 11 June 1961, when West Country 4–6–2 No 34100 *Appledore* headed the train. The next day the Arrow was worked by an electric locomotive.

A new set of Pullman cars was introduced in 1951 for the Festival of Britain. It went into traffic on Monday 11 June with 10 new vehicles built specially for the service: *Aquila, Aries, Carina, Cygnus, Hercules, Orion, Pegasus* (which included the Trianon Bar), *Perseus, Phoenix* and No 303. Two parlour brakes, *Minerva* and No 208, with parlour 35 were refurbished for the service. A feature of the new cars was that the traditional oval shaped windows on the lavatories and pantries were changed to a rectangular shape. They were also the last of the straight-sided Pullmans to be built. The new train, made up at Stewarts Lane, was brought into platform 8 at Victoria to be previewed on the previous Tuesday, 5 June 1951. Just over 30 years later on Tuesday, 11 November 1981 three of those Arrow cars, restored as new, stood again at platform 8, formed up for public viewing of the British component of Sea Containers Orient Express (VSOE) project, the entrepreneurial venture of Sea Containers Group president James Sherwood. The author was present on both occasions, the first in an official capacity, the second time as an interested spectator.

In December 1963 *Pegasus* was withdrawn from the Arrow and went to the London Midland Region, put into the Euston–Glasgow night sleeper to be called the Nightcap Bar. It ran for a while in its Pullman livery, but was later changed to the standard BR blue and grey livery. The car worked for several years until it was replaced by the Hadrian Bar taken out of the Tees-Tyne Pullman. On 14 June 1965 second class Pullman cars were withdrawn from the Golden Arrow and replaced by ordinary coaches. Two years later the management of the service passed to BTH. According to the then prevailing policy the names of the cars were removed and the schedule numbers adopted, though the original names still appeared on the inside of the doors. The livery was changed to the standard blue and grey, staff uniforms were changed and the Pullman job title 'attendant' was redesignated 'steward'. But the greatest and the most far reaching change of all was in the pattern of traffic for, by the late 1960s, the airways and car ferries were creaming off the best. The end of the Golden Arrow came with the last run on Saturday, 30 September 1972. The withdrawal was dignified, nothing as brash as when the Brighton Belle ceased a few months previously. The Golden Arrow service was replaced, rather unceremonially, by ordinary everyday SR electric multiple-unit corridor stock.

Over the years a variety of boat trains ran from Victoria, the gateway to the Continent, including morning and afternoon Boulogne, Calais and Ostend services, and two which deserve special attention. One was the relief Arrow, normally a single Pullman car working, a first kitchen marshalled in the centre of a train of first and third class railway stock. The relief departed 30 minutes before the down Arrow from London, and 30 minutes after on the up journey from Dover Marine to pick up any stragglers. It usually made time on the return so that upon arrival the 30 minute gap between the Arrow and its relief was often quite considerably shortened. The relief was sufficiently important to carry a Pullman conductor. The other boat train to warrant a conductor was the morning Ostend service, once a very popular train. It was usually timed to leave one hour before the Golden Arrow on the down trip and one hour later on the up trip between Victoria and Dover Marine. It was a composite train with two Pullman cars – a first class kitchen, and a bar car, the one-time famous New Century Bar in commemoration of the Belgian Marine centenary – and ordinary SR stock. For many years the impeccable Conductor Pell was in charge of the Ostend service assisted by Bob the Barman, known to thousands of travellers.

The Night Ferry

The Night Ferry, always known to the SR's traffic department as the Dunkerque, provided the only through passenger coaches between Britain and mainland Europe. It was introduced on 14 October 1936 and after the second world war was reinstated on

14/15 December 1947 shortly before the 1948 nationalisation. The daily timings of the reinstated service were:

London, Victoria	dep 20.30	Paris, Nord	dep 20.30*
Paris, Nord	arr 09.30*	London, Victoria	arr 09.10

*French time – one hour later than GMT

In all, 18 type F sleeping cars were built by CIWL for the service, to the British loading gauge, about 1ft narrower and a few inches lower than their mainland counterparts to the Bern loading gauge. The cars were equipped with life jackets and other items needed for a sea crossing. The Ferry was a CIWL and not a Pullman service, though in the late 1930s Pullman cars were included in the make-up to provide a full catering service between Victoria and Dover. In post-war years it had Pullman staffed ROVs. It was an expensive service to operate because of lodging turns. The CIWL personnel had to lodge in London, the Pullman staff overnight at Dover in the old Lord Warden Hotel. It was however a prestige service which had to maintain a certain standard.

From 1947 the Night Ferry was formed in two parts, one with the through first and second class sleepers coupled to an SR ROV two-coach catering set – a buffet bar and a restaurant car – attached to a non-sleeping or walking portion of standard Southern stock with its own buffet car. The ROV two-coach set was marshalled between the two parts of the train, the CIWL sleepers and the SR non-sleeping vehicles. The ROV coach next to the CIWL cars was fitted with adaptor couplings for attachment to the sleeping car couplings, heating pipes and gangways. A spare two-car set similarly adapted was stabled at Grosvenor Road sheds in reserve. It could not be used elsewhere so tied down rolling stock. This did not apply to the other buffet car in the train.

By order of HM Customs & Immigration, access between the two portions of the train was forbidden, hence the provision of two catering units on the train. In practice the Pullman

THE NIGHT FERRY

a la Carte Service

Soup du Jour with Golden Croutons 1/6
Le Potage du Jour

Two Pan Fried Eggs with Grilled Bacon 6/–
Les deux Oeufs sur le Plat avec Bacon

A Plate of Cold Ham with Mixed Salads 9/6
Le Jambon Froid avec Salade Panachée

Ham Sandwich 2/6
Sandwich au Jambon

Grilled Minute Steak 9/6
with
Two Styles of Potatoes and Seasonal Second Vegetables
L'Entrecôte Minute Garni

Fruit Salad and Double Devon Cream 2/6
Le Macedoine de Fruits avec Crème

Cheese Tray 2/6
Les Fromages aux Choix

Pot of Coffee (per person) 2/6
Le Café

Pot of Tea (per person) 2/–
Le Thé

**May we draw your attention to our interesting and
moderately priced Wine List overleaf.**

A la carte supper service on the down Night Ferry 1962.

One of the Pullman stores vans which delivered supplies to services in the London area standing by Battersea Park.

Officers of the Pullman Car Company with Inspector W. Cullen and his group of attendants of various grades and a chef attending a two-day refresher course on car *Corunna* at Stewarts Lane in 1948.

First class parlour brake *Minerva* at Stewarts Lane. It was built in 1927 and remodelled in 1951 for the new Golden Arrow train. Note the rectangular lavatory window fitted at that time. (*Dr A. Hasenson*)

Golden Arrow parlour car *Perseus* of 1951 at Stewarts Lane sidings in 1967. Note the original Pullman coat-of-arms. (*Dr A. Hasenson*)

Pegasus-Trianon Bar at Stonebridge Park sidings near Wembley, as part of the Euston–Glasgow night sleeper 1963, in its original umber and cream livery. It was renamed *Nightcap Bar* and the livery changed to standard BR blue and grey shortly after. (*Dr A. Hasenson*)

conductor could go through from the sleeping into the non-sleeping portion, to see that the second buffet car was under adequate supervision. No stops were allowed between London Victoria and Dover. On arrival at Dover from Victoria, the portions were detached. The sleeping cars were shunted on board the train ferry ship and made secure. The two-coach restaurant/buffet set and non-sleeping portion remained at Dover overnight to be attached the following morning to the inward service. Similar arrangements were made on the French side between Dunkerque and Paris. In 1956 the Night Ferry became a first class only sleeper service; the non-sleeping portion, which frequently ran separately, was unaffected by the change, and at the same time a Brussels sleeping car portion was added to the through portion. The Ferry now served three capitals in true Wagons-Lits style.

The Night Ferry was one of the heaviest trains in Britain, anything from 400 to 600 tons, with from five up to eight sleepers, baggage vans and the SR coaches. The train was usually double headed by two 4–4–0s in its early days, but the Bulleid Merchant Navy 4–6–2s were normally capable of hauling this heavy train single handed. The same applied to the electric locomotives when the line was electrified.

The Ferry was a difficult service to supervise because of the stringent Customs & Immigration regulations. The measures for the prevention of smuggling and illegal immigration sealed off the two portions, the windows of the sleepers were also sealed and so was platform 2 at Victoria, always used by the Night Ferry, to non-travellers. A unique feature of this service was that both Pullman and Wagons-Lits personnel worked on the same train on the British side of the journey. Management supervision was normally performed by any officer or official of either Company travelling on the train.

On 13 May 1948 The Queen, when Princess Elizabeth, accompanied by Prince Philip, travelled to Paris on the Night Ferry on an official visit to the French Capital. The Duke of Windsor, sometimes accompanied by the Duchess, was a frequent traveller. The Duke would usually return by the service

NIGHT FERRY TIMINGS 1978/9. (During GMT in Britain)			
Occupy sleepers from:	21.30	Occupy sleepers on departure	
London, Victoria	dep 22.00	Brussels, Midi	dep 21.32
Paris, Nord	arr 08.40	Paris, Nord	dep 21.25
Brussels, Midi	08.46	London, Victoria	arr 07.45
Vacate sleepers by	08.46	Vacate sleepers by	07.45

on the same day. The visits were private and no official arrangements were made, but the French always held the Duke in high esteem and a Wagons-Lits inspector would discreetly be on the train whenever *Le Prince* travelled.

Sir Winston Churchill also made several trips on the Night Ferry. On one was a unique and historic occasion on Sunday 16 December 1951 when the down Ferry made a special stop at Sevenoaks so that Churchill, then Prime Minister, and staying at nearby Chartwell, could board the train for Paris. It was the only known time that the Ferry made a special stop. Even so, the Customs & Immigration authorities insisted that Sevenoaks station should be closed. Conductor Bew was in charge and his instructions were for a bottle of Dewar's White Label, soda water and cracked ice to be placed in Churchill's sleeping compartment. The Prime Minister returned on the Tuesday night arriving at Victoria on the morning of 19 December 1951.

For the Coronation of Queen Elizabeth II on Tuesday 2 June 1953, the Night Ferry service was duplicated in order to accommodate a CIWL party of 200 travelling from Paris for the occasion. The party was divided into two groups and accommodated in the six sleeping cars in each train. On arrival in London the party was taken by coach to the Thomas Cook stand at Hyde Park Corner. The inward Ferry was retimed and the spare ROV twin-set put into the relief train for the up journey only for breakfast service. The English timings were:

	REGULAR SERVICE	SPECIAL (RELIEF) SERVICE
Dover Marine	dep 03.10	03.35
Victoria	arr 05.00	05.30

Another notable Ferry event was the occasion of the state visit to London in 1958 by the President of the Italian Republic accompanied by Madame Gronchi. At the conclusion of the visit the party left on 16 May by the 22.00 Ferry service. The heavy 14 vehicle train formation was re-arranged for the Presidential party:

2 Brake vans
1 Dining Saloon
6 Sleeping cars, Nos 1, 3, 4, 5 (for Paris) Nos 6 & 7 (to Paris – for Presidential party)
2 Sleeping cars Nos 9 & 10 (for Brussels)
3 Baggage vans

In 1963 the Pullman link with Wagons-Lits was severed when the ROVs were handed over to BTH. In due course the catering vehicles were withdrawn and a substitute service of tray meals and later tea and biscuits, and bar stock, were provided by Travellers-Fare. Towards the end of the 1970s the sleeping cars were nearing the end of their running lives and it was decided the service should come to an end with the last journey from London on Friday 31 October 1980 having plenty of media coverage. Seven blue CIWLT sleeping cars with uniformed BR attendants departed from platform 2, Victoria at 21.25 for the very last time. One of the sleepers, No 3792, has been preserved at the National Railway Museum, York. The end of the last of the great trains, the Night Ferry had survived the Golden Arrow by eight years. The stock from the previous day's inward trip to London returned empty to Paris on the next day, 1 November 1980.

Other Pullmans in Kent
In comparison with the Southern's international services other Pullman workings on the South Eastern Division and its SECR predecessors may seem mundane. A Sunday Thanet Pullman Limited, a first class train, started running on 10 July 1921 from Victoria to Ramsgate. On 31 May 1948 the service was revived as the Thanet Belle, later renamed the Kentish Belle. For the inaugural trip the beauty queens from the various Thanet towns were invited to travel down from Victoria and were met at the

intermediate stops by the respective mayors and other dignitaries. On arrival at Ramsgate there was a civic reception. The Kentish Belle proved to be a moderately successful service and it lasted until the line was electrified in 1959.

Single car workings were introduced about the same time as the Thanet Pullman in the 1920s mainly on business trains, for season ticket holders, the regulars now called commuters. The cars ran between Victoria or Cannon Street and Ramsgate, Charing Cross, Cannon Street, Folkestone and Sandwich, and Charing Cross and Cannon Street to Hastings via Tunbridge Wells, of which the latter must be dealt with separately.

After the second world war, Pullman supplement cars did not return on Kent services other than the Belle. They were replaced by Southern ROV restaurant and then buffet cars, locomotive-hauled and Pullman operated. Later when the lines were electrified the catering vehicles were replaced by buffets, in four-car electric corridor multiple-units classified 4BEP, the first Southern post-war express electric stock. The buffet cars in the 4BEP sets were well-designed vehicles. The kitchen and pantry were combined and with the staff compartment were positioned in the centre of the car. On one side was a bar and on the other a saloon with tables and chairs. This provided a choice of a self service or table service. To provide an adequate service these cars were manned by three staff – one in the bar, one in the saloon and the other in the kitchen. The basic design of these cars was negotiated in 1956 between Eastleigh Southern Region works, where the vehicles were built, and the Pullman Car Company. The essential feature was that the central kitchen/pantry could serve the bar on the one side and the saloon on the other without disturbing the passengers by serving through the bar or through the saloon as is the case when the kitchen facilities are positioned at one end of a vehicle. This design, originally worked out for the buffet cars on the Hastings diesel units of 1957 was adopted for the cars in the electric 4BEPs. The first two fully completed 4BEPs, buffet cars 69000 and 69001 in units 7001 and 7002 respectively were sent to the Central Division in July 1957 as prototypes to be monitored by the CM & EE for two years before the completion of the Kent Coast electrification phase 1 in 1959. The management of the buffets came under the Pullman office in Brighton.

Phase 1 of what was now known as the Ramsgate electrification commenced on 15 June 1959 and Phase 2 on 18 June 1962 when the conversion of the main line via Tonbridge was completed. All boat trains, with the exception of the Arrow and the Ferry, which were both electric locomotive hauled, and other express services were taken over by 4BEP and 4CEP (non buffet) units. All the buffets were ROVs staffed by Pullman. The interchange of rolling stock between Ramsgate, country based and staffed, and London based and staffed, caused a certain amount of difficulties with the buffet cars, particularly in the supervision of the spares. All over the system spare cars were nobody's baby and caused cleaning, equipping and victualling problems when required suddenly for traffic.

Seven days before the introduction of Phase 1, on 8 June 1959 a special train was made up of two 4BEPs with buffet cars 69002 and 69003, in units 7003 and 7004 to convey the Queen and the Duke of Edinburgh from Portsmouth Harbour to Waterloo. Unit No 7004, in the rear, was reserved for the Royal party who travelled in first class accommodation adjacent to the buffet car. The front unit, No 7003, with buffet 69002 staffed, was available to the public. Doubtless the objective was to demonstrate the new rolling stock to the Royal passengers. It was also probably the only occasion a Pullman staffed electric ROV worked on the South Western Division.

Hastings line Pullman cars

Pullman cars started running between London and Hastings via Tunbridge Wells in 1922. The SER line to Hastings suffers from a width restriction between Tonbridge and Bo Peep Junction (St Leonards) because of the narrow tunnels, a legacy of the past. The early cars used on this line were some of the luxury saloon cars purchased by Pullman in 1918 from the SECR and originally built in the USA and at Ashford, during the chairmanship of Sir Edward Watkin. They were bought for the

Hastings American Car Train and the Folkestone Vestibuled Express during the 1890s. The American built cars were shipped in sections and assembled at Ashford.

In 1926 six first class Pullman cars were built by Metropolitan Carriage & Wagon Co for the Hastings line. In 1932 they were converted at Preston Park Works into composite first and third class supplement cars. When on-train catering was resumed after the war, and since the Southern had no catering vehicles within the 8ft body width limit for this line, three of the original composite Pullman cars were put on Hastings services — two in traffic and one spare — as non-supplement refreshment cars. They were converted in 1947 into buffets with half bar and half saloon. The names of the cars *Barbara*, *Madeline* and *Pomona* were replaced by their schedule numbers 182, 183 and 185, but they kept their umber and cream Pullman livery. The other three cars, *Camilla*, *Latona* and *Theodora* were reconverted to firsts and sent to the Pullman pool. Nos 182, 183 and 185 ran until the line was dieselised when all were replaced on 9 June 1958 by ROVs in the new Hastings six-car diesel multiple-units. All the six original Hastings cars in 1958 were then standardised as buffet cars, painted green and sold to the Southern to work in South Western Division boat trains.

THE SIX HASTINGS LINE PULLMANS

Schedule number	Name	Southern number
180	*Camilla*	S7872S
181	*Latona*	S7873S
182	*Madeline**	S7875S
183	*Pomona**	S7876S
184	*Theodora*†	S7874S
185	*Barbara**†	S7877S

* Hastings non-supplement cars 1947–58
† Preserved on Kent & East Sussex Railway

Seven diesel buffet cars were built at Eastleigh to replace the Pullman non-supplement buffet cars on the Hastings line, Nos 60750 to 60756 in units 1031 to 1037. Six cars were in traffic and one spare. These were the first buffet cars of the new centre kitchen-cum-pantry design worked out jointly between the Southern and Pullman later adopted for new electric stock. By the late 1970s and early 1980s many 4BEP buffet car services on the Kent coast were phased out; the Hastings diesel buffets lingered on but were finally withdrawn on 29 August 1980. A few 4BEP buffets continue to operate in selected boat train services.

Pullman specials on the South Eastern
The South Eastern Division had its share of Royal and other specials, but one deserves a special mention here because of its destination on the Hawkhurst branch. It was for the Queen Mother, who visited Cranbrook on Thursday 6 July 1950. The train formation consisted of:
Corridor third brake.
Corridor composite.
Pullman *Malaga*.
Corridor composite.
Corridor third brake.
The Royal visit is commemorated in the Cranbrook town museum. The Hawkhurst branch closed in 1961 and the track was lifted. *Malaga* has been preserved by Ian Allan Ltd at Shepperton.

South Western Division

The Bournemouth Belle

Pullman cars were first introduced on the London & South Western Railway in 1880. They ran variously from Waterloo to Exeter and Southampton and usually as single car workings to Bournemouth until the second world war. On Sunday 5 July 1931 the stately Bournemouth Belle was introduced as a summer service. From 1 January 1936 it ran regularly all year from Waterloo to Bournemouth Central and West, via Southampton West, with a short lived Weymouth portion. The original timings were:

Waterloo	dep 10.30	Weymouth	dep 16.00
Southampton West	arr 11.59	Bournemouth Central	dep 17.10
(later Central)			
Bournemouth Central	arr 12.39	Southampton West	dep 17.55
		(later Central)	
Weymouth	arr 13.00	Waterloo	arr 19.18

When reinstated on 7 November 1946 as an eight to twelve car train – basic seating 74 firsts and 240 thirds – it was retimed to leave Waterloo at 12.30 to Bournemouth Central and West via Southampton Central. In its post-war life the train was normally worked by one of Bulleid's Merchant Navy class Pacifics. But in its closing years the train was usually but not always worked by diesel-electric locomotives. Moreover almost to its last years the Bournemouth Belle included some massive 12-wheel cars. When the Bournemouth line was electrified the Bournemouth Belle withdrew with quiet decorum on 9 July 1967. By this time Bournemouth West had closed and Southampton Central reverted to one of its original names as plain 'Southampton'.

The Devon Belle

The fifth regular post-war Southern 'Belle' service was the Devon Belle, the brainchild of SR general manager Sir Eustace Missenden. The name Belle is always associated with Pullman. It has been given to numerous special trains as well as to regular services. In preservation this practice survives. Only one car, in the life of the Company, was ever called 'Belle', a buffet car built in 1923 for service on the Caledonian section of the LMS, the *Mauchline Belle*.

Sir Eustace Missenden was a great supporter of Pullman, a company in which he took a personal interest. 'A gracious lady in our midst', he said in a speech on the occasion of the launching of 'Pullman's best to the Glorious West' – the Devon Belle, a memorable train. The Devon Belle was a holiday train. It was inaugurated on 20 June 1947 and ran Friday to Monday in the summer timetable. Two trains of up to 12 cars, each train with an observation car, were allocated to the service which ran to Ilfracombe, with a Plymouth portion. The train divided at Exeter Central. There was a locomotive change at Wilton because the Southern had no water troughs, and the train was booked without a public stop to Sidmouth Junction, missing the usual call at Salisbury. The train had a predominance of third class accommodation. The seating capacity of the Ilfracombe portion — excluding the observation car — was 208 of which 138 were thirds. That of the Plymouth portion was 124 of which 102 were third class.

An amusing incident occurred on the down maiden trip of the Devon Belle. As a publicity stunt an actor had been hired dressed in the manner of Sir Francis Drake to travel in the Plymouth portion to participate in a civic reception on arrival. As the train pulled out from Waterloo 'Sir Francis' was seen sitting comfortably in the observation car. A special cocktail was created for the occasion called Spirit of Drake available in this car and served from the miniature bar. All went well until it was discovered that 'Sir Francis' was still in the Ilfracombe portion after the train had divided at Exeter Central. Too much Spirit of Drake? Anyway 'Sir Francis' was bundled into a car at the next stop, rushed by road to Plymouth, overtook the train and arrived just in the nick of time to officiate at the reception. It was customary to create a special drink, usually a cocktail, to toast a new service. Two were created for the Southern's crack new train, the Spirit of Drake just mentioned and a Devon Belle cup.

ORIGINAL DEVON BELLE TIMINGS (1947)		
Waterloo	dep 12.00	
Wilton	arr 13.47	Service stop for loco change
	dep 13.53	
Sidmouth Junction	arr 15.13	
Exeter Central	arr 15.36	

Exeter Central	dep 15.41	Exeter Central	dep 15.48
Exeter St David's	arr 15.44	Exeter St David's	arr 15.51
Okehampton	arr 16.25	Barnstaple Junction	arr 16.49
Tavistock	arr 16.53	Barnstaple Town	arr 16.55
Devonport	arr 17.16	Braunton	arr 17.05
Plymouth Friary	arr 17.36	Mortehoe	arr 17.25
		Ilfracombe	arr 17.32

Ilfracombe	dep 12.00	Plymouth Friary	dep 11.30
Mortehoe	dep 12.12	Devonport	dep 11.47
Braunton	dep 12.23	Tavistock	dep 12.13
Barnstaple Town	arr 12.32	Okehampton	dep 12.45
Barnstaple Junction	dep 12.37		
Exeter St David's	dep 13.31	Exeter St David's	dep 13.21
Exeter Central	arr 13.38	Exeter Central	arr 13.27

Exeter Central	dep 13.40
Sidmouth Junction	dep 14.03
Wilton	arr 15.31
	dep 15.38
Waterloo	arr 17.20

Service stop for loco change

The 27 seat observation cars Nos 13 and 14, built at Preston Park on the underframes of two former kitchen cars were a popular and a novel attraction. After each trip the cars had to be turned, at Ilfracombe and at Nine Elms, since they always had to be the right way round and at the rear of the train.

After 1949 the Plymouth portion of the Devon Belle was discontinued. For the 1954 season the down Devon Belle on Friday was retimed to 16.40, stopping at Salisbury 18.05, Axminster 19.16 and then Sidmouth Junction before Exeter. But the service was not really successful and towards the end there were various alterations of days and train formation. Finally the Devon Belle passed into history after the 1954 season. Yet the Pullman Car Company always used its fleet to the maximum and mid-week the Devon Belle stock complete was used for a series of Cathedral Specials on the Southern organised jointly with Thomas Cook & Son. The observation cars were also used separately before being sold to British Railways and were transferred for use on excursions and summer season holiday services in Scotland and North Wales. Car 13 was eventually bought by the Dart Valley Railway in Devon where it still runs. Car 14 went with Alan Pegler in 1969 to tour the USA with the LNER A3 4–6–2 *Flying Scotsman* and cars *Lydia* and *Isle of Thanet*. The famous Gresley locomotive returned to Britain, but the three Pullmans remained behind for preservation. No 14 now serves as a club bar lounge in San Francisco.

Ocean Liner Services
Pullman operations on the South Western Division based mainly on Waterloo comprised not only the Bournemouth and the Devon Belle all-Pullman services but also the ocean liner boat train specials through Southampton, which were variously part or all Pullman formations. There was also considerable ROV activity but on the South Western Division this did not involve Pullman staff, since other contractors had the concession. Between the wars the GWR, LMS and LNER had their own hotel and catering services, having long since dispensed with any contractors. The Southern was the odd one out. With the exception of a few hotels, including the Charing Cross and the Craven in London, it put hotel and catering services out to contract. Frederick Hotels had the biggest share including the refreshment rooms on the South Eastern and South Western Divisions, the restaurant cars on many South Western Division trains and the railway-owned Channel boats. This contract had previously been held by Spiers & Pond. The refreshment rooms on the Central Division were operated by Bertrams, except for those on the Brighton side of Victoria station which, with the Grosvenor Hotel, were run by Gordon Hotels.

In 1948 the Hotels Executive of the British Transport Commission was formed to take over all railway-owned hotel and catering services. When the BTC was divided into separate entities in 1963 the Hotels Executive became part of a holding company and was redesignated British Transport Hotels. Of the services there were three components – hotels, rooms (the station buffets) and cars (on-train catering). Each component was managed separately but under an overall headquarters and a chairman, board of directors and a general manager. In 1964 the rooms and cars were merged as British Rail Catering; in 1973 this was revamped as Travellers-Fare and from 1 January 1982 T-F was separated from BT Hotels to come under the direct control of BRB – a move which in the opinion of many in the industry should have happened 19 years earlier, in 1963. That then was how railway catering was administered after nationalisation. But back in 1946 the Southern aimed at last to take over the running of its own hotels and catering as the contracts lapsed. It formed its own department and appointed an assistant to Sir Eustace Missenden, the general manager, for hotels and catering. Nationalisation caught up on the project and as the contracts terminated they passed instead to the BTC's Hotels Executive. Catering on the SR boats was an exception as this passed to a marine catering department of the BR Regions as appropriate and later to Sealink.

Thus in the years following the second world war the restaurant car department at Waterloo, located below the station, was managed by Frederick Hotels, soon to be taken within the Hotels Executive. It was large and busy, with the Portsmouth electrics and the West of England services including the crack Atlantic Coast Express and the Royal Wessex to Bournemouth. There were also some boat trains for the Channel Islands, Le Havre and St Malo services, some of which for a brief period were Pullman operated. However, while not involved in domestic services in ROVs on the South Western Division, Pullman was certainly to the fore on Ocean Liner boat trains. The Southern Railway docks at Southampton were a hive of passenger traffic activity, particularly from the 1920s and 1930s to the late 1960s, when the great ocean liners of the world berthed at the SR ocean terminal. Passengers arriving and departing travelled to and from London by special trains. From 1931 onwards most of these trains had Pullman cars in their make-up. A pool of cars stabled at Clapham Junction and Southampton Docks together with a nucleus of staff at each end were allocated to these services. Pullman had an office with an inspector at Waterloo to look after the activities of the South Western Division. As and when required staff were transferred from other parts of the Southern to augment those based at Waterloo and Southampton to work the special traffic boat services.

These special trains were fraught with difficulties; they worked one way only unless there was a balancing service, which was unusual, they were prone to delays, particularly on inward trips, because of unpredictable weather conditions at sea, and were always subject to the many and sometimes unreasonable demands of some of the shipping companies. The trains were made up at Clapham or Southampton as and when required, sometimes lengthy 12-car all Pullman formations, sometimes single cars and sometimes more. Being mostly one way the staff had to travel passenger either down or up, with their stores, to or from their trains.

At one time special trains were supplied to Cunard, United States Lines, P&O, Orient Line, Canadian Pacific, French Line, and other major shipping companies. The then Cunard Steamship Company (originally the Cunard White Star Line) was by far the biggest, post-war fleet including the *Queen Mary, Queen Elizabeth, Caronia, Mauritania, Carmania, Franconia, Carinthia*, and *Sylvania*. For an arrival or a departure of one of the *Queens* three or four trains were needed, the main one being named The Cunarder. For a sailing the first class Cunarder was the last train down from London but for an arrival it was the first train up from Southampton.

For the United States Lines ships *America* and *United States* a similar Pullman train was provided titled The Statesman. On busy days numerous arrivals and departures entailed a constant interchange of Pullman cars and staff, with the drawing up of involved working sheets and complex staff rosters. Yes, you had to know your operating on the Southern!

The importance of these ambassadorial services, as they were called, dealing with tourism and overseas visitors cannot be denied but in practice, despite the prestige, they were seldom financially remunerative. Because of this and the difficulty in providing for one-way traffic with cars and crews sometimes allocated at short notice, it was not always possible to provide a 'Pullman and Perfection' service. One suggested solution was for a permanent Pullman train with a regular crew to be exclusively allocated to this traffic – one wag proposed the name the Golden Fleece! The question then arose as to who would be prepared to subsidise such a train since it could not hope to break even, let alone show a profit. There was much talk but nothing came of the idea.

By the early 1960s travel patterns were changing. Cruises were growing more popular and passengers were going increasingly by air instead of travelling by sea. Buffet cars found more favour in meeting the needs of cruise passengers than first class Pullmans. Some of the buffets were Pullman non-supplement vehicles, others were ROVs – as for example the six former Hastings cars now railway owned and dressed in Southern green livery.

On 1 January 1963 the BTC was wound up and control of the railways passed to the British Railways Board with Doctor Richard (later Lord) Beeching as chairman. It was also the day that Pullman became a Division. On Thursday 13 June of that year the last Pullman-operated boat train service ran on the South Western. After that date all ocean liner traffic was worked by ROVs under the control of the restaurant car manager, Waterloo. That last Pullman service was a composite train with *Ibis*, *Cassandra* and *Argus*, and ordinary SR coaches for the United States Lines.

A regular train service to an airport such as between Gatwick and London, Victoria, on the Southern, or Reading on the Western, is now taken for granted but an airways Pullman service would be regarded as unusual. Yet an Airways Special between Victoria and Christchurch for Hurn Airport, and to Bournemouth West for the Poole flying boat base ran during the second world war. The train included ordinary stock and up to four Pullman cars. It was mainly a link with trans-Atlantic flights and usually ran on an as required basis and often at short notice. Chief Inspector Badger acted as conductor and Claude

James looked after the catering. The Airways and the other special wartime trains and work kept the Pullman depot at Battersea ticking over throughout the period of hostilities. An Airways regular was President Franklin D. Roosevelt's special envoy Harry Hopkins. It was on one of these visits that Pullman nearly put a spanner in US aid to Britain. During the height of the U-boat campaign at one of the blackest periods of the war, food supplies were running low in Britain. Winston Churchill appealed to Roosevelt for assistance and the President dispatched his special envoy to England to deal with the situation. Churchill travelled down on the Airways train to meet Harry Hopkins and on the return the two men got down to business over dinner on the train. But back in London a very angry Churchill lost no time in contacting Pullman Chairman Stanley Adams. It transpired that after Churchill had been pressing the point that Britain was on the brink of starvation and urgently needed more food supplies, Harry Hopkins praised the food on the train saying it was the best meal he had eaten for a very long time!

Royal and State specials
A very happy event took place at Waterloo station on Thursday 20 November 1947 when a Royal train ran to convey Princess Elizabeth and Lieut Philip Mountbatten on their honeymoon. The train formation was:
    Corridor third brake
    Corridor composite
    *Rosemary**
    Rosamund
    Corridor third brake
    *Royal car
On Wednesday 29 July 1981, 34 years later, and well out of the Pullman era, another honeymoon train ran from Waterloo to Romsey for the Prince of Wales and his bride Lady Diana Spencer, now Princess of Wales. They also were going to Broadlands. The train was made up of three vehicles, a BR Mark 1 brake composite, a Mark 2 corridor first and the SR general

manager's saloon No TDB 975025 – itself rebuilt from a one time Pullman-operated Hastings demu buffet S60755 – acting as the royal car. Yet there was another Pullman connection, for it was staffed by Travellers-Fare including chief steward Jimmy Meylan from the royal train, and chief steward Ron Turner, formerly with the Pullman Car Company working on the Brighton Belle.

Sir Winston Churchill died in London on Sunday 24 January 1965 and was given a state funeral on the following Saturday, 30 January. Sir Winston had requested to be buried at Bladon by Blenheim Palace, his birthplace. His body was taken by train from Waterloo station to Handborough, on the Western Region, the station nearest to Bladon. A special private train of Pullman cars was formed up at Stewarts Lane to be worked by Battle of Britain locomotive No 34051 *Winston Churchill*, from Nine Elms Shed. After the service at St Paul's Cathedral, and the river trip from the Tower of London to Waterloo Pier the cortège was met by a bearer party from the Queen's Royal Irish Hussars who carried the coffin at Waterloo station and placed it on board the bogie van marshalled in the special train. The formation was:

No 208	BL
SR Bogie van 2464	
Carina	KT
Lydia	KT
Perseus	P
Isle of Thanet	BT

The bogie van had been painted in Pullman umber and cream livery to match the Pullman cars.

Geraldine, one of the cars used on the 1924 Kings Cross–Sheffield service. It was later converted to *Third Class Car No 166.* The then current livery with cream carried to the cantrail above the windows is distinctive. *(LNER)*

Hastings line 8ft wide non-supplement buffet car No 185, originally built as *Barbara* in 1926. *(G. M. Kichenside)*

Joan at St Pancras in 1962. It had been sent over from the SR to the LMR for inspection by former President Eisenhower who had used it in the second world war. *(BRB)*

Brighton Belle unit No 3051 including first class cars *Hazel* and *Doris* on the Quarry Line near Merstham. (*Lens of Sutton*)

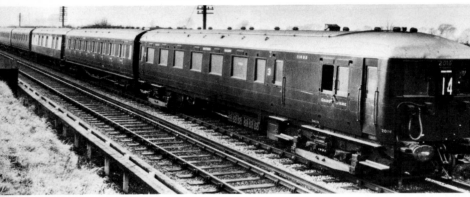

One of the SR's 6PUL units, seen here when new with its original unit number 2016 (later 3016) with composite car *Iris* on a trial trip from London down the Brighton line. (*L&GRP*)

It was quite a feat to get a four-seat first class coupé, eight seat first class saloon, kitchen, pantry, 16-seat third class saloon and a toilet compartment in the SR's Brighton line composite cars in the 6PUL units. This is *Enid* from the ill-fated unit 3014 involved in two collisions in 1948 and 1958.

5 Pullman on the Eastern

THE regular Pullman activities on what in 1923 became the LNER and in 1948 the Eastern Region of British Railways were on the Great Northern out of Kings Cross and the Great Eastern Railway from Liverpool Street.

The Great Northern was among the pioneer Pullman users with sleepers and parlour cars in the 1870s, but its main claim to fame was the running of the first regular restaurant car in which meals were prepared and served on board on a British railway in 1879. This was in the specially converted Pullman car *Prince of Wales*. Pullmans continued to operate on the GNR until 1895/6. They were to return in the 1920s after the formation of the LNER. By then though Pullmans had already spread to the Great Eastern Railway where they remained until the outbreak of war in 1939. The general manager of the GER in the early 1920s was American, Sir Henry Worth Thornton, late of the Pennsylvania Railroad, who was reputed to have known George Mortimer Pullman, which may well have accounted for the presence of Pullman cars on the GE.

Pullman services on the GER were based on Liverpool Street Station. The first cars ran on boat train services to Parkeston Quay and Harwich for Hook of Holland, Flushing, Antwerp and Zeebrugge. By 1923 in addition to the boat trains, Pullman cars also ran on services to Cambridge, Clacton, Cromer, Harwich Town, Hunstanton, Ipswich, Lowestoft, Norwich, Southend and Yarmouth. However the LNER and the Pullman Car Company were not convinced of the viability of Great Eastern section Pullman services and renegotiated the contracts in which most of the GE Pullmans disappeared but new long distance Pullman trains were introduced on the GN main line. Not all the GE

Pullmans were withdrawn; they survived on boat trains from Liverpool Street and a complete Pullman train, the Eastern Belle, worked excursions to various East Anglian coast resorts and was also used as a race train to Newmarket. During the summer period the Eastern Belle ran to different destinations on different days of the week and passengers sometimes booked a package of trips for the week. Most of the services were popular and remunerative though there was some doubt about the boat trains where Pullman had been obliged to compete with the railway's own restaurant cars.

After the second world war Pullmans were no longer seen on the Great Eastern section except on two occasions. On 15 September 1962 a private special train with *Lydia* and *Argus* conveyed President Tubman of the Republic of Liberia from Southampton Docks to Parkeston Quay, a journey which took $4\frac{3}{4}$ hours leaving at 15.32 and arriving at 20.15. The second occasion was for the Crown Prince of Japan on 27 October 1965. A Pullman car was put at his disposal in a service between Liverpool Street and Harwich.

The Great Northern and East Coast route was the line for the big time Pullman services from the 1920s. By the end of 1958 four long distance Pullman trains still ran from Kings Cross — the Master Cutler, Tees-Tyne Pullman, Yorkshire Pullman and Queen of Scots, which also operated into Scotland. The Yorkshire Pullman and the Queen of Scots were products of the between-the-war years but the Tees-Tyne and the Cutler were relative newcomers. All four were crack trains running on good timings and loading well. The Pullmans were usually worked by one of Gresley's Pacific classes or in post-war years by the Peppercorn A1s or Thompson A2s. When steam was in the process of being phased out in the late 1950s and early 1960s the Master Cutler was the first service to be diesel hauled. The age of the famous Deltics was at hand.

It was about 40 years earlier, on 9 July 1923, that the Harrogate Pullman, a four car train, went into service on the LNER and brought Pullmans back to the GN main line after an absence of nearly 30 years. It worked out of Kings Cross to Leeds

Central, Harrogate, Ripon, Darlington and Newcastle. It was extended to Edinburgh on 2 July 1925 and for the first time two trains were required to cover a service. A six-car Sheffield Pullman was introduced on 2 June 1924 between Kings Cross via Nottingham to Sheffield. On 12 July 1925 it was re-routed via Retford, and was extended to Manchester to become the Sheffield & Manchester Pullman but it was short lived, for in September 1925 the service was withdrawn and put on to a Kings Cross to Leeds and Bradford run with, in 1926, a car to Halifax. This service was named the West Riding Pullman. Around this time too a Sunday Harrogate Pullman was introduced. In 1935 with the addition of a Hull portion, detached at Doncaster, and a Bradford portion to Halifax detached at Leeds, the West Riding was renamed the Yorkshire Pullman.

The name Harrogate Pullman which in 1925 was extended beyond Harrogate to Scotland was really a misnomer and it acquired the unofficial title of the Edinburgh Pullman, but on 1 May 1928 the situation was regularised and the Harrogate Pullman became the Queen of Scots.

At the same time the Pullman cars operating on the Great Northern were replaced by new all-steel cars built by the Metropolitan Carriage & Wagon Co. This 1928 build of 30 cars is rated among the finest and best appointed vehicles owned by the Pullman Car Company. The Queen of Scots service then settled down to operate on its regular route from Kings Cross via Leeds to Edinburgh and then on to Glasgow calling at Leeds, Harrogate, Darlington and Newcastle.

At the outbreak of the second world war the LNER Pullman services ceased to run; 30 cars were loaned to the LNER for the duration and were painted in teak livery; the balance was stored on sidings on the Southern Railway.

One car, *Joan*, from the 1928 batch of all-steel cars, was used for journeys by the King and Queen and also for Winston Churchill. It later spent the rest of the war in a train with a sleeping car for the Chiefs of Transportation of the US Army. It became known as General Ross's car, was based at his

91

QUEEN OF SCOTS
FORMATION OF TRAIN FROM KINGS CROSS

	Car		Seats	
A	Second	Parlour	42	Leeds Portion
B	First	Kitchen (trailing)	20	
C	Second	Parlour Brake	30	Glasgow Portion
D	Second	Kitchen (trailing)	30	
E	Second	Parlour	42	
F	First	Parlour	24	
G	First	Kitchen (leading)	20	
H	First	Kitchen (trailing)	20	
J	Second	Parlour Brake	30	
		Total Seating	258	

QUEEN OF SCOTS – TIMINGS (1963)

No 1 Train
From Kings Cross Mondays,
Wednesdays and Fridays.

No 2 Train
From Kings Cross, Tuesdays,
Thursdays and Saturdays

Kings Cross	dep 12.00
Leeds (City)	arr 15.14
	dep 15.22
Harrogate	arr 15.52
	dep 15.55
Darlington	arr 16.42
	dep 16.45
Newcastle	arr 17.25
	dep 17.30
Edinburgh (Waverley)	arr 19.35
	dep 19.45
Falkirk (SD)	20.17
Glasgow (Queen Street)	arr 20.40

No 1 Train
From Glasgow Tuesdays,
Thursdays and Saturdays.

No 2 Train
From Glasgow Mondays,
Wednesdays and Fridays

Glasgow (Queen Street)	dep 11.00
Edinburgh (Waverley)	arr 11.53
	dep 12.00
Newcastle	arr 14.02
	dep 14.09
Darlington	arr 14.52
	dep 14.55
Harrogate	arr 15.43
	dep 15.46
Leeds (City)	arr 16.19
	dep 16.30
Kings Cross	arr 19.45

(SD) Calls required to set down passengers from Newcastle and south thereof; if call was made at Falkirk arrival at Glasgow was 5 minutes later.
Timings of the Queen of Scots were altered on occasions since the 1928 inauguration of the service.

Cheltenham headquarters, ran all over the country and as far north as Gourock in Scotland. For its war service the car was awarded a special commendation. On its return to civilian duties *Joan* went back to Kings Cross and later to the Southern. As far as can be ascertained it was sent for scrap in 1967.

A new Pullman service was introduced on 27 September 1948, the Tees-Tyne Pullman, which ran from Newcastle to Kings Cross. The service called at Darlington in each direction with an additional stop at York on the down run. A special feature of the Tees-Tyne was the Hadrian Bar. The fourth Pullman train to be introduced on the Eastern Region was the Master Cutler on 15 September 1958, 10 years after the Tees-Tyne. The Master Cutler — the name revived from the one time express, not a Pullman, on the LNER's Great Central route — was country based and made four trips between Sheffield and Kings Cross. The formation is of interest since it is predominantly first class:

	CAR	SEATS
A.	Second Brake	30
B.	First	20
C.	First	20
D.	First	20
E.	First	20
F.	Second Brake	30
	Total	140

The Monday to Friday timings are equally interesting since they run through all the meals of the day — breakfast, luncheon, afternoon tea and dinner.

Sheffield (Victoria)	dep 07.20
Kings Cross	arr 10.05
	dep 11.20
Sheffield (Victoria)	arr 14.15
	dep 15.20
Kings Cross	arr 18.15
	dep 19.20
Sheffield (Victoria)	arr 22.05

At that time this was intensive use of stock, SR fashion, but today found all over BR. A single Pullman crew worked all trips but rosters were arranged so that each man only worked four days out of the five.

With faster running towards the end of the 1950s, the 1928 cars were in need of replacement. An order for 44 new cars was awarded to Metropolitan-Cammell (successor to the Metropolitan Carriage & Wagon Co); delivery commenced in 1960 and was completed in 1961. The cars were basically similar to the BR Mark I type and were fitted with Commonwealth bogies, suitable for 100mph running; schedule numbers were 311 to 354. Of the 44 cars 21 were first (13 kitchens and eight parlours with 20 and 24 seats respectively), and 23 second class (15 kitchens and eight parlours, 30 and 42 seaters respectively). One car, No 354, included a new Hadrian Bar, schedule number 354, with 24 seats. It replaced the old bar car converted from 1928 car No 59. No new parlour brake vehicles were built; existing cars instead were refurbished to match, as far as possible, the new cars. The 44 Metro-Cammell cars are now historic inasmuch as they were the last umber and cream Pullmans to be built, the only ones to use the profile of the BR Mark 1 coach body and not straight sides as in the 1951 Golden Arrow cars, and because the majority have been preserved. The 1928 cars displaced by the 1960 Metro-Cammell cars were sent to the Southern where, in turn, they replaced older cars marked for conversion into camping coaches.

Following the creation in 1963 of the Pullman Division one of the first changes on GN line services was the reintroduction of the Harrogate Sunday Pullman, on Sunday 16 September 1963, between Kings Cross and Harrogate with a Bradford portion detached at Leeds. The service was made up from the London based Queen of Scots. There were now five Pullman limited trains on the Eastern Region.

Pullman on the Eastern

SUNDAY HARROGATE PULLMAN – 1963 – FORMATION

	Cars		Seats	
A	Second	Parlour	42	Bradford Portion
B	First	Kitchen	20	
C	Second	Parlour Brake	30	Harrogate Portion
D	Second	Kitchen	30	
E	Second	Parlour	42	
F	First	Parlour	24	
G	First	Kitchen	20	
H	Second	Parlour Brake	30	

Timings were:

Down		Up	
London, Kings Cross	dep 09.40	Harrogate	dep 15.23
Doncaster	arr 12.55	Leeds City	arr 15.52
	dep 12.56	Bradford (Forster Square)	dep 15.25
Leeds City	arr 13.57	Leeds City	arr 15.46
	dep 14.13	Leeds City	dep 16.02
Bradford (Forster Square)	arr 14.34	London, Kings Cross	arr 20.00
Harrogate	arr 14.34		

However travel patterns were changing and in particular against competition from the airways between London and Scotland; the loadings of the Queen of Scots centred around Leeds and Harrogate to and from Kings Cross. On 13 June 1964 the service was discontinued. In its place, two days later a new Pullman service, with an old name – the White Rose – an eight-car train, went into traffic between Kings Cross and Leeds.

London, Kings Cross	dep 12.20	Leeds	dep 16.40
Wakefield	arr 15.00	Wakefield	dep 16.56
Leeds	arr 15.20	London, Kings Cross	arr 19.40

On 7 September in the same year the departure was altered to 11.20 and the service, still using one set of cars and staff, was extended to Harrogate. As a service the White Rose did not last very long, for it was taken off after the Saturday running of 4

March 1967, at the same time as its offspring, the Harrogate Sunday Pullman finished after its last run a day later.

In June 1964 organisational changes within British Rail Catering began to have effect. With the objective of developing its Pullman acquisition by taking advantage of its specialist expertise a number of important restaurant car circuits on the Eastern, Midland and Western Regions were transferred at intervals to the Pullman Division. This was an unusual departure. Hitherto, as on the Southern ROV were only passed to Pullman management when they replaced Pullman cars. Now ROVs were to be allocated to Pullman from the restaurant car departments of the Regions concerned. The Kings Cross to Edinburgh Talisman was the first service to be thus transferred on 14 June 1964. Two sets covered the service, one Eastern, the other Scottish Region based. One was made into a composite train with the first class accommodation provided by Pullman cars and the seconds with ordinary stock with a Pullman staffed ROV restaurant car. The balancing train was made up of standard stock with restaurant car. The Pullman cars though were taken off in the following April.

On 12 July 1946 the West Riding service – no relation to the pre-war West Riding Pullman – 07.45 Kings Cross to Leeds and 07.30 Leeds to Kings Cross, with associated workings, were taken over. This was followed by the 10.00 Flying Scotsman to Newcastle and Edinburgh and 10.00 Edinburgh (Waverley) to Kings Cross, one of the oldest named trains on BR dating back to 1862, and the 14.00 Kings Cross to Edinburgh (Waverley) Heart of Midlothian and all allied workings on 6 September 1964. The Heart of Midlothian had been inaugurated in Festival of Britain Year, 1951. On 4 October 1964 the 10.20 Kings Cross to Leeds and the 09.00 Kings Cross to Newcastle and return workings were passed to the Pullman Division. Other services such as the 07.25 Leeds, 11.00 and 12.00 Kings Cross to Edinburgh and the 18.05 North Eastern also came into the Pullman orbit. The catering on all the ROVs on these services was by Pullman and the BR staff transferred with their cars into the Pullman Division. In addition to all the ROVs there were, by March 1967, still three Pullman trains on the Eastern Region, the Yorkshire, Tees-Tyne and the Master Cutler.

At that time another more far reaching management reorganisation was about to take place. On 14 March 1967 the Pullman Division ceased to be operative and the control of all Pullman managed services passed to the group restaurant car field manager responsible for the Eastern Region. Second class cars were withdrawn and the seating in the firsts increased. The firsts lost their names, but retained their schedule numbers prefixed by a letter E. The cars were painted in the standard blue and grey BR livery. The seven 1960 second class parlours from the 44 Metro-Cammell build were converted to standard open firsts, put back into traffic in BR livery and ran until 1980/81. The Master Cutler was withdrawn on 4 October 1968. The Yorkshire Pullman and the Tees-Tyne Pullman were made into composite trains, with first class Pullmans and second class ordinary standard BR stock. From 6 March 1967 the Hull portion of the Yorkshire Pullman ran as a separate composite train as the Hull Pullman and the Tees-Tyne Pullman was discontinued. Pullman services continued for another decade but on Friday 5 May 1978 the last scheduled Pullman services left Kings Cross for their respective destinations of Harrogate and Hull.

In commemoration of the passing of East Coast Pullman services, a jointly sponsored railtour of first class Pullman cars was organised for 20 May 1978 by the DAA Railtour Society, the Diesel & Electric Group, and Travellers-Fare. The special East Coast Pullman Farewell train departed Kings Cross at 08.30 and ran via Peterborough, Grantham, Doncaster, Wakefield, Leeds, and Harrogate to York. After passengers visited the National Railway Museum, the special continued via Malton, Scarborough (run-round), Filey, Bridlington, Beverley, Anlaby Road Junction, Goole, Doncaster, Retford, Newark, Grantham, Peterborough and Kings Cross arriving at 21.45. It was the end of an epoch. Pullman services were replaced by Inter-City HSTs and the cars went for preservation. The emphasis had changed. Instead of having a top rung Pullman style first class the BRB upgraded the ordinary first and second class accommodation, with air conditioning and fitted carpeting for all. Formal meals were still served at appropriate times but the much faster journeys meant that conventional meal service was not always needed. Thus the self service buffet with call-order fast food at the buffet counter was now becoming the fashion.

6 Pullman on the Western

THE Great Western Railway and its Western Region successor after nationalisation in 1948 always retained its fierce pride. For Pullman, the Great Western was the scene of both failure and triumph. Not just failure but devastation; not only triumph, but unqualified success. Indeed the Pullman story on the Great Western is almost one of rags to riches.

In 1929 Pullman negotiated a contract to introduce Pullman cars on the Paddington–Plymouth ocean liner trains from May, serving the French line – Compagnie Générale Transatlantique, Cunard White Star and other shipping lines. On 8 July in the same year an eight-car Torquay Pullman went into traffic between Paddington, Torquay and Paignton. The timings were:

Paddington	dep 11.00	Paignton	dep 16.30
Newton Abbot	arr 14.25	Torquay	dep 16.40
Torquay	arr 14.40	Newton Abbot	dep 17.00
Paignton	arr 14.50	Paddington	arr 20.30

The Pullman intrusion on the GWR though was resented right from the start. Matters were made worse by the fact that the general manager, Sir James Milne, an autocratic but distinguished railwayman in the GWR mould, and the then chairman of the Pullman Car Company disliked each other. Constant operating difficulties were put in the way of the cars and staff at Old Oak Common and, particularly, at the country end. Here, stolid Devonian railwaymen, taking a lead from their management, deliberately feigned to misunderstand the somewhat complicated operating and servicing requirements of Pullman cars in the makeup of trains and their running. Matters were made even worse when the GWR introduced its own Torbay Express on better timings and a faster schedule than the Pullman. There were no supplementary charges and the on-train catering was as good as on the Torquay Pullman. This was no surprise. The GWR hotels and catering department was skilfully managed by R. A. P. Setterfield, formerly of Cunard White Star and a specialist in his field. The unpopular Pullmans were literally run off the road and all were withdrawn in 1930. Why the Great Western agreed to run the Pullmans in the first place if it did not really want them is a mystery.

It was fortunate for the Pullman Car Company that at about this time Southampton was developing as an ocean liner seaport which could handle larger ships than Plymouth. The displaced Pullman cars from the GWR were transferred to the South Western Division of the Southern for the new ocean liner trains and also for the proposed Bournemouth Belle. These developments on the friendly Southern Railway were fortuitous and helped Pullman to recoupe some of its GWR losses of face and finance.

To the GWR cataclysm there is a sequel. The Great Western lost no time in building its own vehicles modelled on Pullman lines for the coveted Plymouth boat traffic. It named these vehicles after members of the Royal Family. *Queen Mary, King George V*, and took fullest advantage of the fact that Great Western livery resembled Pullman umber and cream. Indeed these super-saloons were frequently mistaken by the public for Pullman cars. The Pullman style armchairs, the table lamps – even the supplement – were all there. Moreover the GWR ocean saloons were 1ft wider than the Pullmans, taking advantage of the wider loading gauge of the GWR's former broad gauge routes. If the Great Western could copy the rolling stock it was also capable of emulating the on-board service with its well trained restaurant car staff.

The South Wales Pullman
When 25 years on, in 1955, it was proposed to introduce another Pullman service on the Western, the news was received with

incredulity by the long serving members of the Pullman Company, many of whom once retreated with their cars from the dreaded GWR. But the 1955 climate differed from that of 25 years back. The GWR was now a Region of BR, and the BTC had a controlling interest in the Pullman Car Company. Moreover, Keith Grand, the Region's former general manager and by then a member of BTC, and F. D. M. Harding were on the best of terms.

The new train was the Paddington-based South Wales Pullman inaugurated on 27 June 1955. It departed 09.55 arriving Swansea 14.00 after calling at Newport, Cardiff, Port Talbot, and Neath. It returned at 16.35 arriving Paddington 20.45. The service was normally worked by Great Western 4–6–0 Castle class locomotives. A special SWP feature was the Daffodil Bar with an attractive lady attendant in Pullman uniform. The bar was installed in the 1928 car *Diamond* which had reverted to its original name. Traditional GWR pride was still there but this time it was turned to Pullman's advantage. No difficulties were encountered in mounting the service. The Pullman Car Company received splendid co-operation from the highly professional Western Region. The South Wales Pullman was a success and nothing succeeds like success.

In view of what happened in the past it is portentous to record what occurred in April 1957. Because of industrial action at Southampton the Cunard liner *Queen Mary* was prevented from docking, and since no other port on the South Coast could accommodate the great liner she remained at Cherbourg. Here the passengers for Britain were transferred to the smaller Cunard ship *Ivernia* and taken to Plymouth where the Cunarder train, sent over from Southampton, was waiting to take the passengers to Paddington (not Waterloo via the Southern route, be it noted!). The Pullman boat special on 2 April was made up of nine cars: *Montana, Argus, Hawthorn, Juno, Rosamund, Phoenix, Rainbow, Valencia* and *Seville*.

Two days later three boat specials with Pullman cars, including the 09.40 Cunarder, ran from Paddington to Plymouth Millbay Docks where the process was reversed. The passengers boarded the *Ivernia* and were taken to Cherbourg to join the *Queen Mary* bound for New York. The entire operation was with the full support and co-operation of the appropriate Western Region departments including the restaurant car staff. It went without a hitch. Certainly the past was more than vindicated for, on that morning of 4 April 1957, Paddington station was full of Pullman cars. But more was to come.

The Blue Pullmans
It was in 1955 that Sir Brian (later Lord) Robertson the BTC chairman announced his £1,200 million modernisation plan for British Railways. Apart from general dieselisation and some electrification there were to be three new Pullman services, one for the London Midland and two for the Western Region. The objective was to demonstrate to the public the shape of things to come and the new Pullmans were to be fixed formation diesel-electric multiple-units painted in a striking new livery of Nanking blue and white. The Blue Pullmans were to be air-conditioned and sound-proofed, with wall-to-wall carpets, double-glazed windows and an altogether modern luxury interior in which industrial designers produced styles never seen before on a British train. The cars were carried on Metro-Schlieren bogies following Swiss practice, but they did not prove to be as good under the heavy Pullmans compared with the excellent ride under Swiss lightweight stock.

The first meeting between the Pullman Car Company, the British Railways planners and Metropolitan-Cammell Carriage & Wagon Company took place in August 1956. Four years later, in 1960, the Blue Pullmans went into traffic. The London Midland service was a six-car first class only train, called the Midland Pullman, running between Manchester and St Pancras; the Birmingham Pullman and the Bristol Pullman on the Western were eight-car first and second class trains.

One particular problem revolved around the staffing of the services. The National Union of Railwaymen expressed fears that its restaurant car members would be displaced by these Pullman staffed services. The Pullman Car Company already had an agreement with the NUR and Pullman train staff were encouraged to join their union. It must be admitted though that the majority of Pullman staff were far more Company than union minded. In addition to the agreements with the NUR for car staff, Pullman recognised the Transport Salaried Staffs' Association (TSSA) for the supervisory and clerical grades, and the National Union of Vehicle Builders (NUVB) for the works. There was no agreement with the British Transport Officers' Guild for the management grades and so far as it can be ascertained there were only two members of BTOG – the works manager and the author. Preston Park Pullman works staff were called out on strike by the NUVB in 1948 because of a national dispute. This delayed the re-introduction of the Queen of Scots and took a long time to live down within the Company. Union trouble was encountered when Pullman ventured back on to the Midland with the Blue Pullman but this is dealt with in the next chapter.

The staffing problems on the Western were solved when it was agreed that vacancies on the new trains would be advertised in the Region's restaurant car department, and that BR seniority would be respected and all privileges honoured. Once again scepticism was expressed in the Pullman camp about this working out. The doubters need not have worried, for the restaurant car grades – conductors, chefs, and attendants recruited and transferred to Pullman for the blue trains were excellent material and quickly settled down to the Pullman way of life of which they were to become very proud.

To work the three Blue Pullman services 36 cars were required; 24 firsts (including 10 kitchens) and 12 second class. Four of the firsts were driving cars with the diesel power plant, and six of the second class cars. The cars were not given running names but had BR standard numbering prefixed, as appropriate, by the letter W or M. The cars were given Pullman schedule numbers 555 to 590, the last vehicle to appear on the official 1960 list.

The railway numbers for the 24 Western cars were:

W60044 to 60049	W60734 to 60739
W60094 to 60099	W60744 to 60749

Three eight-car sets of 228 seats – 108 firsts and 120 seconds – were required for the Western trains, two for traffic and one set spare.

As for the interior details, the double glazed windows had inset Venetian style blinds between the panes, lighting was fluorescent, and the traditional Pullman table lamp was there, but of an ultra modern design; seating was of the adjustable airline type arranged two + one at tables for four and two in both classes, a breakaway in the firsts from the previous single armchairs at tables for two in most first class cars. Like all Pullman trains at that time the sets were equipped with a public address system. The kitchens, which were in the 18 seat first class cars, one in each four-car half train, were fitted out in stainless steel and plastic, with refrigerators, deep freeze cabinets and twin sterilising sink units. The stoves made to specification by Radiation of Warrington were bottle gas fired and equipped with incandescent grills and a cast aluminium branders, but other equipment was electrically powered. All the food and beverage service equipment, cutlery, plate, glassware and crockery was specially designed and manufactured. Later this new equipment was extended to most other Pullman trains. Menus and the tariffs were also specially designed for these new trains. Also featured was a redesigned Pullman coat-of-arms both on the external body panels and for internal decor, menu headings and table appointments. This also was extended to all Pullman services replacing the one originally introduced by Lord Dalziel. The coat-of-arms, incidentally, embodies the heraldry of England, Ireland, Scotland and Wales. It is said that Lord Dalziel's ambition was to obtain the Royal Warrant in which case the Pullman coat-of-arms could be surmounted by a crown. The new design of 1960 was at the personal interposition of Sir John Elliot. The name of the service together with the destinations were carried on roller blinds positioned on each side

Leading Attendant Hawkes of the Golden Arrow prepares his car for traffic
ready to receive the travelling public. Note the special Arrow lapel badges
and the blue shoulder cords of rank. (*Dr A. Hasenson*)

F. D. M. Harding OBE, managing director, Pullman Car Company with
two of his conductors at the inauguration of the Midland Pullman on 1 July
1960. Conductor (designate) Walton in white jacket and gold cords with
Conductor Pearte in blue uniform who was seconded to the service for
instructional duties. (*BR, LMR*)

One of the six-car diesel Blue Pullman units for the Midland Pullman service on a trial run in 1960. (*Metro-Cammell*)

Four members of Pullman staff from Brighton seconded to the Midland Pullman for the trial, demonstration and inaugural runs in 1960. Apart from the dramatic new livery of Nanking blue and white, new style serif lettering and a new coat of arms were all details emanating from the industrial design team responsible for the modern styling. (*BR, LMR*)

of the front and rear power cars.

When the units were standing at their regular siding berths and also at their terminal stations they were plugged into a shore electricity supply so that the 1,000hp diesel generators could be shut down. This was done not only to conserve fuel but at stations for noise abatement. The shore supply provided lighting for the train and power for the electrically powered kitchen equipment. Precautions had to be taken to ensure that power cables were disconnected and secured before the train moved off. The Midland Pullman went into traffic first on 4 July 1960. The two Western services, the Birmingham and Bristol Pullmans followed on 12 September 1960. All three services were country based and on Mondays to Fridays, covered four trips. All the sets were available on Saturdays for special party traffic.

BIRMINGHAM PULLMAN

		From 11.9.61
Wolverhampton (Low Level)	dep 07.00	
Birmingham (Snow Hill)	dep 07.30	
Solihull	dep 07.40	
Leamington Spa (General)	dep 08.00	
London, Paddington	arr 09.35	
London, Paddington	dep 12.10	dep 10.10
Leamington Spa (General)	arr 13.34	arr 11.34
Solihull	—	—
Birmingham (Snow Hill)	arr 14.10	arr 12.05
Birmingham (Snow Hill)	dep 14.30	dep 13.00
Solihull	—	—
Leamington Spa (General)	dep 14.55	dep 13.25
London, Paddington	arr 16.30	arr 14.55
London, Paddington	dep 16.50	
Leamington Spa (General)	arr 18.19	
Solihull	arr 18.44	
Birmingham (Snow Hill)	arr 18.55	
Wolverhampton (Low Level)	arr 19.20	

From 11 September 1961 middle trips re-timed earlier as above shown.
The train was stabled at Cannock Road sidings.

BRISTOL PULLMAN

	From 12.9.60	From 11.9.61
Bristol (Temple Meads)	dep 07.45	dep 08.15
Bath Spa	dep 08.02	dep 08.32
Chippenham	—	—
London, Paddington	arr 09.35	arr 10.10
London, Paddington	dep 10.05	arr 12.45
Chippenham	arr 11.29	arr 14.09
Bath Spa	arr 11.45	arr 14.25
Bristol (Temple Meads)	arr 12.00	arr 14.45
Bristol (Temple Meads)	dep 12.30	dep 15.15
Bath Spa	dep 12.45	dep 15.32
Chippenham	dep 13.00	dep 15.49
London, Paddington	arr 14.25	arr 17.15
London, Paddington	dep 16.55	dep 17.45
Chippenham	—	—
Bath Spa	arr 18.25	arr 19.20
Bristol (Temple Meads)	arr 18.45	arr 19.40

Notes: For the summer timetable in 1964 middle trip was experimentally extended to Weston-Super-Mare.

The train was stabled at Dr Day's siding.

SOUTH WALES PULLMAN – from 11 September, 1961.

Swansea (High Street)	dep 06.40	London, Paddington	dep 16.55
Port Talbot (General)	dep 07.03	Newport	arr 19.02
Bridgend	dep 07.19	Cardiff (General)	arr 19.20
Cardiff (General)	dep 07.50	Bridgend	arr 19.49
Newport	dep 08.08	Port Talbot (General)	arr 20.08
London, Paddington	arr 10.15	Swansea (High Street)	arr 20.40

Notes: Monday to Friday service.

From 7 September 1964 a middle trip was put on to Cardiff: Paddington dep 11.00 Newport arr 13.02, Cardiff arr 13.20. Return Cardiff dep 14.30, Newport dep 14.45, and Paddington arr 16.50. Depart Paddington for fourth trip 17.40 and arrivals retimed accordingly.

On 11 September 1961 the spare eight-car set went into traffic, Swansea based, as the new South Wales Pullman. It replaced the London based locomotive-hauled service. All three Western Region 90mph diesel-electric Blue Pullman sets were now in regular service. It was a bold move and a characteristic one. It illustrated the maximum utilisation of rolling stock and the reluctance of having thousands of pounds worth of equipment standing idle on sidings.

With no spare eight-car diesel set problems arose. The original theory was that being new and well tested the units would require only light maintenance. This could be carried out overnight or during layovers. Heavier work could be performed at weekends. From the outset the British Rail and the Pullman operating staff, always cautious, doubted very much if this theory would work in practice. As usual they were right. It was soon clear that after extensive running major servicing and overhauls would be needed and each set had to be taken out of service in rotation. Some problems were unforseen, as for example when a member of a gang working on the track near Swindon accidentally left a jack in the path of the Bristol Pullman fracturing one of the fuel tanks. A standby train of orthodox locomotive-hauled Pullman cars was assembled in the November at Old Oak Common to be used as a spare as and when required for any of the eight-car sets taken out of traffic. It was immediately nicknamed 'Wells Fargo' after the popular TV Western horse opera series of the time. The name stuck so hard it almost became official.

The first standby was a nondescript train:

CAR	SEATING
A	30
B	30 (K)
C	42
D	42 (K)
E	42
F	30 (K)
G	30
TOTAL	246

This eventually became standby No 1, as another train was required. The formation of standby No 2 was the same but the cars were not numbered. The seating arrangements were left to the conductor. Even though the Wells Fargo cars, which in order to provide an adequate number of seats, particularly the two + one of the Blue Pullman firsts, were second class cars, later refurbished, renovated and given names, they made an unfavourable contrast with a Blue Pullman set and this brought many passenger complaints.

The building of a spare eight-car diesel-electric set was ruled out on economic grounds but would certainly have paid off if complaints could have been costed out. But something had to be done. The problem was not solved until 1966/7 when traffic to West Midlands and Manchester was concentrated on Euston with the completion of the initial London Midland Region electrification scheme. The WR decided to reallocate the Blue Pullman sets and to withdraw the Birmingham Pullman service. Moreover the two London Midland Blue Pullman sets were also then spare. There would then no longer be a need for a Wells Fargo standby.

The cars which were allocated to, modified and given running names for standby trains circa 1964 were:

Pullman Schedule	New Running Name	Former Running Number	Type
188	*Avon*	66	P
226	*Ceteia*	73	P
210	*Hebe*	105	K
227	*Melandra*	74	P
215	*Severn*	60	K
211	*Thalia*	106	K
216	*Thames*	61	K
212	*Thetis*	107	K
193	*Wye*	35	P

Note: The rake of cars was planned to be interchangeable between Western and London Midland regions.

Cars 105, 106 and 107 originally *Marcelle, Sybil* and *Kathleen*, converted in 1946 from firsts to thirds were built in 1927. Car 61

(*Thames*) survived the Wells Fargo standy legend; cars 35 (*Wye*) and 105 (*Marcelle/Hebe*) went for preservation, the balance were sold for scrap when the Fargo set was withdrawn. The fact that *Thetis* was the name of an ill-fated Royal Navy submarine seems to have passed unnoticed. The boat while on trials in the Thames Estuary sank in June 1939 with loss of life. Later she was raised, refitted and renamed HMS *Thunderbolt*. In 1943 she was sunk by enemy action. None of the standby names appear on any Pullman schedule.

Members of the Royal Family seldom travelled Pullman except on the Southern. There were exceptions, as on 1 November 1961 when the Queen Mother travelled to Birmingham on the 10.10 Birmingham Pullman.

The Birmingham Pullman made its last run on Friday 3 March 1967. As the train pulled out of Paddington at 16.50 the driver gave two long blasts on the horn, a *cri-de-coeur*, the end of a service. The crew of the Birmingham was transferred over the weekend to a new Pullman-staffed service which entered traffic on the LMR's new electrified West Midlands main line on Monday 6 March 1967. It was a locomotive-hauled train of restaurant cars and standard BR stock, known as the Executive Express and departed Wolverhampton (High Level) at 07.30 to Euston, returning at 17.50. The formation was:

Electric locomotive	
Corridor Brake First	
2 Corridor Firsts	
2 Open Firsts	2x42
Kitchen	—
Open First	42
Kitchen	—
2 Open Seconds	2x48
2 Open Seconds	
Brake Van	

Though Pullman operated it was not a Pullman train, but there was a reservable first and second class restaurant section for which supplementary fares were charged – 7s 6d (37½p) first and

4s (20p) second class – Pullman fashion. The 1967 meal prices were: full breakfast, served on the up trip 10s 6d (52½p) with light breakfast 6s (30p); three-course dinner, served on the down journey was 14s 6d (72½p) with 1s (5p) extra for coffee.

The Pullman-operated Executive was an experimental service to test the market. But that Monday, 6 March, was an eventful day for the Pullman Division still part of a ring organisation of British Rail Catering. Not only did it see the introduction on the LMR of the Executive but also two new Pullman car services on the Western – a London based South Wales Pullman and an Oxford Pullman. The eight-car set displaced from the Birmingham Pullman formed the London based South Wales service. Both South Wales Pullman trains, one based at Swansea and the other in London, were now worked by eight-car sets. The Oxford Pullman was formed of one of the six-car Blue Pullman sets, with a proportion of first class seating converted to seconds, from the Midland Pullman service withdrawn a year previously on 16 April 1966. It was intended as a middle of the day working for one of the units employed on the Bristol Pullman. The other six-car set, with first and second seating, went as the Bristol Pullman on the middle of the day run, both units coming up from Bristol to Paddington in the morning and going back to Bristol on a down early evening service. They replaced and released the third eight-car set which was now spare. It was considered that an eight-car set was now justified as a spare cover for all the Blue Pullman services on the Region.

The Oxford Pullman departed Paddington 12.15 arriving Oxford 13.15. It departed Oxford again 16.15 arriving at Paddington 17.15. The service, though, failed to attract the anticipated tourists in sufficient numbers and was short lived. If the service had been based at Oxford or beyond it might at that time have done better with commuter traffic. The new London based South Wales departed Paddington 09.00 arriving Swansea (High Street) 12.20. It returned at 16.20 arriving Paddington at 19.00. The train called each way at Newport, Cardiff (General), Bridgend and Port Talbot.

As on the Eastern Region, after the Pullman Division was set up in 1963, by arrangement with the chief of refreshment rooms and restaurant car services from 1 November 1964, Pullman took control of catering on the Plymouth based Golden Hind and the Paddington to Swansea Capitals United. There were no difficulties here as by now Pullman was well accepted in the Western Region. Three more restaurant car circuits were planned to follow – the Mayflower, Red Dragon and the crack Bristolian – but they did not materialise.

Despite the introduction of new Pullman services on 6 March 1967 when so many timetable changes occurred, it was really the beginning of the end for only week later, 13 March 1967, came Pullman's last day. The following day, control of Pullman's Western Region assets passed to the field manager, restaurant cars, Paddington. The Bristol Pullman and the South Wales Pullman continued to operate into the early 1970s until they made way for the 125mph HST Inter-City 125 sets for which in many ways the blue trains had blazed the trail.

7 Pullman on the Midland

THE first Pullman cars to work on a British railway operated on the Midland Railway. The last Pullman cars in regular British Rail service worked on the London Midland Region. The first cars were assembled at Derby works of the Midland Railway. The last British Pullman cars were built at the Derby workshops of British Rail. The wheel has thus turned full circle. The cars on the Midland Railway worked from 1874 until 1888, and 72 years were to pass before Pullman cars returned to St Pancras station. The Midland Pullman – one of the Blue Pullman services described in the previous chapter – was introduced in 1960 on the London Midland Region with almost as much trepidation as the locomotive-hauled South Wales Pullman was on the Western Region in 1955. As on the Western, so on the Midland, the staff for the Blue Pullman were recruited from the Region's restaurant car department. Negotiations between the parties concerned and the NUR were conducted on very formal lines and the terms of the agreement strictly adhered to. There were no qualms about the quality of the staff recruited from the Region's restaurant car department, for they were most professional. Special dispensation had to be negotiated with the NUR for a cadre of Pullman staff to be sent over from the Southern and Western Regions to act as instructors in initiating the newly transferred staff to the Midland Pullman service. Until 1960 the Pullman Car Company was able to move its staff freely between the BR regions. As soon as BR restaurant car staff were recruited this freedom of movement ceased and train staff were confined to their regions. Union agreement thus had to be sought to move any member of the train staff from one region to another.

The two six car units were brought into St Pancras for

114

equipping and inspection on 14 and 15 June 1960. The BR numbers of the 12 cars in the two units were: M60090-93; M60730-33; M60740-43. On 1 July both six-car sets were used, one country and the other London based, for separate inaugural trips with invited guests which included mayors, civic dignitaries and senior rail officers. The timings were:

Manchester Train

| Manchester (Central) | dep 11.35 | Derby | dep 12.55 |
| Derby | arr 12.49 | Manchester (Central) | arr 14.09 |

London Train

| St Pancras | dep 11.45 | Leicester (London Rd) | dep 13.20 |
| Leicester (London Rd) | arr 13.10 | St Pancras | arr 14.47 |

Identical arrangements were made for luncheon on both trains. The Midland Pullman crew, augmented by regular Pullman staff, worked the Manchester train and staff drawn from other regions, mainly the Southern, worked the London train.

The Midland Pullman went into traffic on 4 July 1960. It was a Monday to Friday only service covering four trips:

MIDLAND PULLMAN – from 4.7.60	
Manchester (Central)	dep 08.50
Cheadle Heath	dep 09.04
St Pancras	arr 12.03
	dep 12.45
Leicester (London Road)	arr 14.10
	dep 14.33
St Pancras	arr 16.00
	dep 18.10
Cheadle Heath	arr 21.07
Manchester (Central)	arr 21.21

à la carte service

Fruit Cup Cocktail Cerisette 1/6
Crème Mongole with Golden Croûtons 1/6

Fruit Juices
Pineapple 1/6   Tomato Cocktail 1/6   Orange 1/6

*Rainbow River Trout Amandine 8/6
*Chicken à l'Américaine 8/6

From the Grill
*Fillet Steak Garni Princess 12/6   Lamb Chop 8/6

**Price includes*
Parsley & Lyonnaise Potatoes   Braised Celery Hearts   French Beans
Garden Peas

The Chef's Cold Collation 8/6

Royal Trifle Chantilly 2/–

Cheese Tray
Cheddar   Wensleydale   Camembert   Gorgonzola 2/–

Coffee 8d.

Bread Basket of White and Hovis Rolls
Ryvita and Curled Butter 6d.

In any difficulty will passengers please send for the *Conductor*.
Failing satisfaction, please write to the
Managing Director, Pullman Car Co. Limited, Victoria Station, London, S.W.1,
enclosing your bill.

The main meal à la carte service on the Midland Pullman.

The following year because the train loaded lightly on the middle trip it was decided, as from 2 October 1961, to extend it to Nottingham calling additionally at Loughborough. The service was retimed accordingly with a 07.45 departure from Manchester on the first trip.

MIDLAND PULLMAN – from 2.10.61	
Manchester (Central)	dep 07.45
Cheadle Heath	dep 07.59
St Pancras	arr 11.00
	dep 11.20
Nottingham Midland	arr 13.20
	dep 15.45
St Pancras	arr 17.45
	dep 18.10
Cheadle Heath	arr 21.07
Manchester (Central)	arr 21.20

Note: Called at Leicester and Loughborough on the middle trips.

The retiming however ran into problems, for the NUR saw it as an extension of Pullman operations which of course it was, and to which the union was totally opposed. The previous year at its annual conference in Blackpool a resolution was passed for the NUR executive to work for the abolition of Pullman services and their assimilation into the hotel and catering services of British Transport. The Pullman Car Company was, at the time, largely controlled by the British Transport Commission but the preference shares were still privately owned. It was to this that the NUR objected, for it did not want any profits to go outside the BTC and Pullman was a profitable business.

The upshot was that on Monday 2 October 1961, on arrival at St Pancras from the 07.45 Manchester, the attendants walked off the train and only returned for the 18.10 service back to Manchester. The conductor and the chefs remained on the train but only to perform essential services. The Pullman management was shocked! It was the first time in the recorded history of Pullman in Britain that car staff had refused to work a service. News of the strike was widely reported in the media; one national newspaper actually recalled the 1893 Pullman City strike and that if George Mortimer Pullman were still alive he 'would not be surprised' because 'he had his full share of labour trouble'.

For the first few days the train ran as booked. Pullman supervisory and clerical staff covered the middle trips to deal with the supplement tickets and seeing to the doors. But as no catering could be featured and because what amounted to strike breaking ran the risk of wholesale Pullman blacking, the Nottingham run was withdrawn until such time as the dispute could be settled. Eventually it was resolved and normal working resumed on 30 November 1961. It was all the more unfortunate since the staff were good, and had earned the respect of the Pullman management. But they were steeped in union lore. It was thought that the correct consultation procedures had not been carried out regarding the extension and retiming of the service. Pullman clearly had something new to learn. A six-car set was used occasionally on Saturdays on special charter. On one occasion it was to Aintree for the Grand National on 21 March 1964 and on another on 2 May 1964 for the FA Cup Final at Wembley when West Ham United beat Preston North End 3-2. The Midland Pullman ran for six years until 16 April 1966 when the staff were transferred to the new electric Manchester Pullman from Euston, of which more later.

As on the other regions several restaurant car circuits were transferred to Pullman Division management on the London Midland at Euston. Already mentioned in the previous chapter, the Executive between Wolverhampton and Euston was worked by former WR Birmingham Pullman men. Between March and May 1965 the Division took on six LMR circuits: The Red Rose (Liverpool), Emerald Isle (Holyhead), Shamrock (Liverpool), Merseyside (Liverpool), the Liverpool Riverside boat trains, and the 18.05 Euston Mancunian. Almost at once came union opposition and though it emanated from a minority and was unofficial it was an irritant. The main cause of the trouble seemed to be the Pullman insignia, the use of the coat-of-arms on menus and tariffs which one attendant, presumably transferred against his will, described as a 'badge of shame'. Matters had to be smoothed to avoid disruption to services by industrial action over a storm in a teacup. The powers that be decided it prudent to adopt the new BR double arrow logo in place of the Pullman coat-of-arms. This took the heat out of the situation. It will be recalled that the BR logo was introduced on 1 January 1965 along with the designation British Rail, and when with the new look package, including uniforms and signs, railwaymen became railmen. Was it also then that passengers became customers and the travelling public, the market? At the end of 1965 the 24 hour clock was brought in.

The Electric Pullmans

The big break on the LMR came when having acquired full control of Pullman British Rail was anxious to develop the potential of its acquisition. This opportunity came with the introduction of the first phase of the London Midland Region's mammoth 25kV overhead electrification scheme in 1966. As part of the proposed 100mph Inter-City service there would be included Pullman trains between London, Manchester and Liverpool.

The cars were to be all first class and locomotive-hauled, and four return trains were scheduled to run 'under the wires'. The Manchester Pullman service consisted of two eight-car trains of 240 seats, one London, the other Manchester based. The Liverpool Pullman service consisted of two composite trains of four Pullman cars, giving 120 seats, attached to standard BR second class stock with a Pullman staffed miniature buffet. One Liverpool set was to be based in London and the other at Liverpool. As for stock, 29 new cars would be required, 24 in traffic and five spare. The cars were not named but given BR numbers:

8 kitchen cars of 18 seats, M500-7
14 parlour cars of 36 seats, M540-53
7 parlour brakes of 30 seats, M580-6

The cars were of BR Mark 2 type built at Derby and painted in silver and blue livery. The cars were fully air-conditioned and soundproofed, the first Mark 2 stock so equipped, but following their diesel Blue Pullman predecessors, to which they were similar in internal decor and fittings. Additional staff, following the established procedure, were recruited from the region to augment the nucleus transferred from the Midland Pullman. The trains went into traffic on Monday 18 April 1966 and quickly became established.

ORIGINAL TIMINGS OF THE EUSTON–MANCHESTER and EUSTON–LIVERPOOL PULLMAN

MANCHESTER PULLMAN

Euston	dep 07.50	Manchester	dep 07.50
Manchester	arr 10.27	Euston	arr 10.25
Manchester	dep 18.00	Euston	dep 18.00
Euston	arr 20.36	Manchester	arr 20.36

LIVERPOOL PULLMAN

Euston	dep 07.45	Liverpool	dep 07.55
Liverpool	arr 10.24	Euston	arr 10.30
Liverpool	dep 18.00	Euston	dep 18.10
Euston	arr 20.46	Liverpool	arr 20.46

These services, which later ran on various timings, proved to be the last regular Pullman trains on BR. Eventually the Liverpool was withdrawn, and only the Manchester Pullman remained at the time of writing.

MANCHESTER PULLMAN 1982/3

LONDON TRAIN		MANCHESTER TRAIN	
Euston	dep 07.56	Manchester, Piccadilly	dep 07.35
Stockport	—	Stockport	dep 07.43
Manchester, Piccadilly	arr 10.27	Euston	arr 10.05
Manchester, Piccadilly	dep 16.42	Euston	dep 17.00
Stockport	—	Stockport	arr 19.22
Euston	arr 19.13	Manchester, Piccadilly	arr 19.30

It is the only all first class train on BR. The service is scheduled to run until such time as it is replaced by the next generation of rolling stock.

The Manchester Pullman sets are much in demand for charter at weekends and appear under many named promotions and usually, if not always, as a Belle or a Pullman.

To commemorate the centenary of Pullman car operation in Britain, and its own jubilee, the Locomotive Club of Great Britain chartered a special train of London Midland Region cars on 29 June 1974. On this occasion it was named the Clyde Coast Pullman and ran from Euston to Glasgow and return via Gourock on the newly electrified line to Scotland and was operated by Travellers-Fare.

8 Pullman in Scotland

AT one time or another Pullman cars have run over most of the main lines in the United Kingdom and on a number of branch lines. Cars began running through to Scotland from the Midland Railway and the Great Northern Railway as early as 1876. Two American-built Pullman sleeping cars of 1883, *Balmoral*, and *Dunrobin*, later renamed *Culross*, were transferred from the GNR in 1885 to the Highland Railway where they worked until 1907. Surprisingly they ended up at the other end of the country as dwellings at Seaford, Sussex. Unusually, they were without the end balconies which characterised Pullmans of that period.

Pullman services really started in Scotland in July 1914 when a 20 year contract was signed with the Caledonian Railway. In all some 19 cars were allocated to the Caledonian, and the Glasgow & South Western Railway, and an office was opened in Glasgow. The services continued to operate, apart from the first world war years, until 1933 when the cars were sold, and the staff transferred, to the London Midland & Scottish Railway to come under the control of Arthur Towle's LMS Hotel Services.

The 10 original cars built by Cravens of Sheffield for the Caledonian contract were well named:

Annie Laurie	*Mary Beaton*
Fair Maid of Perth	*Mary Carmichael*
Flora MacDonald	*Mary Hamilton*
Helen MacGregor	*Mary Seaton*
Lass O'Gourie	*Maid of Morven*

With the exception of the observation car *Maid of Morven*, which was an eight-wheeled car, the rest were twelve-wheeled buffet cars. They ran variously between Glasgow and Edinburgh to Aberdeen, Perth, Dundee, Oban, south to Carlisle and to

Until 11 June 1961 the Golden Arrow was steam-hauled, although for short periods diesels had been used. Thereafter it became an electric locomotive duty. BR standard Pacific No 70004 *William Shakespeare*, one of the two members of the class allocated for this duty in the 1950s heads the train through Tonbridge. (*G. M. Kichenside*)

Monday 12 June 1961, the first official day of electric locomotive working on the Arrow, with Class 71 Bo-Bo No E5015 at the head. The leading Pullman is *Isle of Thanet*. (*Kent & East Sussex Courier*)

Scene at Kings Cross on 27 September 1960; the newly-built Metropolitan-Cammell cars formed in the Master Cutler are being inspected by British Railways and Pullman Car Company senior officers. (*BR, ER*)

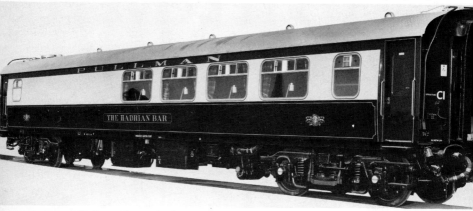

Before: Second class parlour car *Hadrian*, No 354 of the Tees Tyne Pullman. It was one of the 44 Metropolitan-Cammell cars. Note the redesigned Pullman coat of arms as on the Blue Pullmans. (*Metro-Cammell*)

After: The *Nightcap Bar* formerly the *Hadrian Bar* carrying its revised schedule number as M354E and BR livery stands at Stonebridge Park sidings. In 1980 the car reverted to its original nomenclature and is owned by the Steam Locomotive Operators Association. (*Dr A. Hasenson*)

other destinations. In the summer, excusions were run between Glasgow and Oban with *Maid of Morven* in the make up of the train 'operating over a route probably unsurpassed in the world for its beautiful scenery'.

In 1923 other vehicles joined the Scottish fleet on the Caledonian section of the LMS including the eight-wheeled dining cars *Meg Dods, Lass O'Ballochmyle* and the buffet *Mauchline Belle*. It will be noted how many of these Pullmans allocated to Scotland carried long names. In later years lengthy names were ruled out since they would be far too costly on paint and transfers.

The cars in Scotland sometimes ran as supplement and at other times as non-supplement buffet or restaurant cars. Towards the end of the contract conflicting prices were charged for catering facilities provided by the LMS restaurant cars, the Glasgow operated Pullmans and the Pullmans on the main line to Scotland from Kings Cross, the Scottish worked Pullmans being higher! This reflected upon the Pullman management in London. One of the more unusual sights to be seen in 1931 on the 17.30 Glasgow to Carlisle train was a Pullman car coupled to a through Glasgow-Penzance GWR coach. After 1933 the cars, now owned and worked by the LMS, continued in service as restaurants and buffets until 1938 when they started to be withdrawn for breaking up.

On 12 July 1925 the Harrogate Pullman was extended to Edinburgh from Kings Cross. The service was next extended to Glasgow in May 1928 and at the same time was renamed *Queen of Scots*. This train survived except during the second world war until 1964 as the only regular Pullman train in Scotland after 1933, although as we have already seen one of the Devon Belle Pullman observation cars ran on the Kyle line from the late 1950s but not under Pullman control.

On Tuesday 16 October 1962 an unusual event occurred in connection with the official visit to Scotland of King Olav of Norway. The Scottish Region wanted to put on a special show. Impressed by the part played on the Southern by Pullman they wanted similar arrangements for King Olav. Metro-Cammell cars *Hawk* and *Pearl* were formed in a train for the short journey from Leith to Edinburgh, Princes Street. F. D. M. Harding travelled with the railway party and Chris Lade was the Pullman conductor in charge.

9 Pullman in Ireland

IN 1926 Lord Dalziel negotiated a contract with the Great Southern Railway of Ireland. Four third class Pullman cars, Nos 100, 101, 102 and 103, went into service between Dublin Kingsbridge (today's Heuston), Limerick and Cork and later extended to Sligo. The cars were specially built by Birmingham Carriage & Wagon Company and were shipped minus their 5ft 3in gauge bogies which were supplied by the LMS. These were the only British-built Pullman cars not of standard gauge.

A special company to operate the Irish cars was formed, Pullman Car Company (Ireland) Limited. By all accounts the Irish operation was a leisurely affair and officers from London took turns in going to Dublin to look after the Pullman office. It was a popular and an enjoyable duty. The contract terminated in 1936, the cars were sold to the Great Southern Railway which continued to operate them. Indeed they were still in service when Coras Iompair Eireann took over control in 1945 of the GSR and other railways in what became the Republic.

In 1947 a contract was awarded to Gordon Hotels Limited to operate CIE hotel and catering services. The franchise consisted of six hotels, station refreshment rooms and restaurant cars, including the former Pullman vehicles. John Ennis, appointed by Gordon Hotels to manage the Irish contract was seconded to the Pullman Car Company for a period of time with the object of studying on-train catering operations at first hand.

In 1950 exploratory talks took place about the possibility of a Pullman train running an elite service between Dublin and Cork, but the negotiations did not come to anything.

10 The Cars

THERE is something personal about a Pullman car. To travel Pullman was an occasion. In preservation it becomes a rarity. Each car developed a personality. Every car has an individual history. How many cars in Britain passed through the Pullman stock books? This is no easy question to answer with accuracy because of gaps in the history of the Company. Valuable records were destroyed during the London blitz in the second world war when the Pullman offices at Victoria Station were damaged on four occasions by fire and high explosives. Matters are also complicated by the profusion of alterations, conversions, renaming and renumbering of vehicles which relentlessly took place over the years. With works at Preston Park, Brighton and offices in London one suspects that clerical errors could, on occasion, have occurred with records. With all this in mind the total number of cars can only be estimated at 455. This number is made up as follows:

The 1960 Pullman Car Company schedule of cars dating from 1876 (84 years): 390; in 1966 further cars built at Derby for the London Midland Region electrification: 29; the balance represents the estimated number of cars operating between 1874 and 1876: 36 (of which 11 were sleeping cars).

The 1960 list used as the basis for this book is a re-scheduled list and may well conflict with (but cancels) all previous lists (if they exist). The schedule does not include cars built in Britain by Pullman for CIWL and not returned and nor any of the ROVs operated by Pullman on any railway or region. There are some discrepancies in building dates on this schedule which may and does cause confusion. Vehicles purchased from railway sources are shown with the year of purchase and modification and not the original date of build. The eight cars built in 1925 for CIWL, Italy, are shown as 1928 build, the year in which they were returned to the UK and modified. More significant is the fact that some of the 30 cars built in 1928 for the LNER are dated 1929 and the 1951 Golden Arrow cars are listed as 1952. Possibly some of the 1928 and 1951 cars were not taken on the books and/or delivered until a year later, or, more likely, the Company, ever conscious of the age of its cars, wanted to show them off in the youngest light. In July 1966 the Pullman Division published a list of 153 cars which included the 29 London Midland locomotive-hauled vehicles but excluded any building dates or schedule numbers. By this time the Division had been in existence some three years and seemed to take notice only of running names or numbers of vehicles actually in working order and available for revenue earning service. But even in Company times schedule numbers were of far more interest to the engineers and to the accountants than to the commercial (marketing) departments which particularly favoured named cars and named trains. When the British Railways asserted itself the Pullman vehicle schedule numbers were prefixed E for Eastern, M for Midland, S for Southern, Sc for Scottish and W for Western Region. The Pullman Division did not publish a list of ROVs it operated on the Eastern, Midland and Western regions, the numbers of which are estimated at about 25; as for the Southern it is calculated that after the second world war the Pullman Car Company operated in total some 60 ROVs.

A curious feature of the Pullman fleet was its variety of cars and the initial lack of standardisation. It was a mixed bag of vehicles. The different types of vehicles and their builds together with non-standard seating often played havoc with train formations, seating and booking plans. The Company worked its cars and they had to earn their keep. The objective was to maintain the maximum number of cars in revenue traffic and for as long as possible. One example of this policy was the 1908 *Grosvenor* which ended its regular service in the Newhaven boat train. Even after 52 years service it still had its uses as a camping coach on the Eastern Region before finally suffering the indignity of the breaker's yard.

There were five classes and types of Pullman cars:

A. A *first class* car could either be a kitchen, parlour or a brake.
B. A *third class* car (re-classified to *second class* from 3 June 1956) could also either be a kitchen, parlour or a brake.
C. For a brief period, before 1956, there were a few *second class* dining cars on the books (basically for the three class SR continental boat trains).
D. A *composite car* comprising half first and half third/second class accommodation and was usually a kitchen car.
E. An *unclassed car* was usually a bar car with access to passengers of both classes of travel. The whole car could be a bar, or the bar could be sited in a first or second class vehicle. The *Devon Belle* observation cars were unclassed and non-supplement vehicles.

Seating varied in locomotive-hauled cars and with some exceptions was calculated at 20 and 24/26 for first class kitchens and parlours respectively, and 30/32 and 42 for third/second class vehicles.

In the 44 Metropolitan-Cammell 1960 cars the seating was standardised at:

	Firsts	Seconds
Kitchens	20	30
Parlours	24	42
Bar	—	24

The 29 BR, Derby 1966 first class cars for the LM electric service had seating of:

	Firsts
Kitchens	18
Parlours	36
Brakes	30

The original British Pullman cars were built in the USA, until about 1908. The last Pullman cars were built in 1966 at BR's Derby works. Between there were some five main contractors: Birmingham Carriage & Wagon Company; Cravens of Sheffield; Clayton Wagons of Lincoln; Midland Carriage & Wagon Company; and Metropolitan Carriage & Wagon

Company which in 1930 became the Metropolitan-Cammell Carriage & Wagon Company.

Many vehicles were bought from various railway services and converted or modified; others were built at the Pullman works at Longhedge and at Preston Park. After the first world war about 22 redundant ambulance coaches were bought from the railways and converted into Pullman cars. Always appreciative of a bargain, Lord Dalziel acquired these vehicles at a competitive price and after conversion put them to revenue earning principally on the developing Continental traffic and on the Kent coast commuter services.

The early cars were built entirely of wood with heavy wooden underframes, or with bodies having massive timber framing formed of cantilever trusses built into the sides to produce a self-supporting structure – integral construction in today's terms.

By the 1920s wooden frames had given way to steel underframes and in 1928 came the all steel car. Wooden bodied cars with steel underframes were often given a face-lift by being plated over by steel sheets which improved appearance and prolonged the life of the car. The American cars were characterised by their clerestory roofs which after 1908 were replaced by the standard eliptical roof.

Technical details varied and reproduced here is a random sample of eight separate types:

Date	Type	Builder	Tare Weight Tons	Length	Width	Nos Built	Notes
1914	Caledonian *Maid of Morven*	Cravens	43	63' 10"	9' 0"	9	12 wheels
			43	59' 4½"	8' 11"	1	8 wheels
1926	SR Hastings Line	Metro C & W	39	57' 1½"	8' 1"	6	—
1926	Ireland	Birmingham C & W	39½"	57' 1¾"	8' 11"	3	5' 3" gauge

1928	LNER	Metro C & W	37/41	63' 10"	8' 7"	30	all steel cars
1932	Brighton Electrics Motor brake cars	Metro Cam	43 66¾	66' 0"	9' 0"	} 38	—
1951	Golden Arrow	Birmingham C & W/ Pullman	38/40	63' 10"	8' 5½"	10	—
1960	Eastern Region	Metro Cam	38/40	64' 6"	9' 0"	44	—
1960	Blue Pullmans Power Car	Metro Cam	33/49 67½	65' 5½" 65' 6"	9' 0" 9' 0"	} 36 —	— —

If the Company spread its building programme over several carriage and wagon firms it was rather more conservative in awarding contracts for car interiors, furnishings, carpets, upholstery, panels and heavy duty kitchen equipment. The principal car furnishings were from W. Turner, Lord & Morison & Company of London and Edinburgh, Maple & Company, and Waring & Gillow of London and Manchester. Kitchen car *Pauline* built in 1924 by Midland Carriage & Wagon, decorated and furnished entirely by Waring & Gillow was described thus:

> The whole interior is panelled throughout in mahogany with black band and light lime border panels, which have floral and ribbon marquetry with oval inlaid medallions bearing a classic figure. The pilasters are inlaid with light lines and the moulded cornice crossbanded with light and dark lines. Green trellis carpet and light ground floral moquette on chairs. The fittings are of gilt, and the complete scheme reflects the careful thought and experience brought to bear on the problem of securing a pleasant combination of appearance and comfort.

Pauline was later converted to third class and given its schedule number 171. The carriage fittings including toilets were by James Beresford of Birmingham. Kitchen plant and equipment suppliers were W. M. Still of Hastings and stoves by Radiation of Warrington and their predecessors. J. Stone & Company of Deptford supplied electrical equipment. Kitchen equipment was a particularly specialised area, for the plant, besides being serviceable also had to be durable and capable of withstanding heavy use and the shocks and strains of travel.

Cooking on cars was originally by solid fuel. Gas was introduced in 1908 and electric cooking in 1932/33 with the Brighton electrification. The gas was an oil gas under pressure carried in cylinders on the underframe of the kitchen cars. Gas was manufactured by the railways at a number of plants and transported to terminal points by cylinder rail trucks. Oil gas had been in general use for lighting on railway-owned coaches from the 1870s but by 1905 had started to give way to electric lighting, although gas lighting and cooking from oil gas did not disappear until the early 1960s. Oil gas was expensive but bottled gas, first seen in the 1950s, was cheaper. It was Pullman which introduced bottled gas (Propane) to the railways for cooking purposes but not until it won quite a sustained fight against the conservative elements on the railways. It meant the closure of gas plants, scrapping of cylinder trucks and the conversion of vehicles from oil to bottle gas. The large gas bottles were carried in banks of two on the underframe – one in use, the other in reserve. Electricity on the Southern, taken from the third rail through a high tension line along the train, was metered and again was expensive. When the Blue Pullmans, which generated their own power, were built, Pullman opted for bottle gas cooking which was under its own control.

It can be speculated that Lord Dalziel knew Sir John Blundell Maple, MP, head of the great furniture firm, who financed the formation of Frederick Hotels. The chairman of Frederick's was the legendary hotelier Frederick Gordon who also formed Gordon Hotels. Lord Dalziel did business with Maple & Company. On his travels he often stayed at the Royal Pavilion Hotel, a Frederick Hotel, by Folkestone Harbour, in preference to the Metropole on the Leas at Folkestone, a Gordon Hotel. From his suite at the Royal Pavilion, armed with binoculars, his

Lordship could observe how his Pullman cars loaded on the boat trains. He could also check that the staff were at the doors of their cars. There is no record that the Pullman chairman did the same at Dover, staying at the Lord Warden, a Gordon Hotel on the harbour in preference to the Burlington, a Frederick Hotel, on the seafront.

Throughout its history, Pullman is credited with a long list of firsts: the first vehicles to be carried on bogies (although this really needs a qualification – the first standard gauge coaches on bogies, 1874, since the narrow gauge Festiniog Railway just beat Pullman in 1873); the first to have vestibules and connecting gangways which gave enclosed communication between cars in 1888; the first to be steam heated; the first to be lit by electricity 1881; the first to be fitted with buckeye interlocking couplers and a system of continuous braking 1874; the first kitchen/restaurant car with on-board meal preparation 1879; the first to have full air-conditioning 1960; the first to have cooking by bottle gas, and many other innovations. In August 1948 a portable bookstall service was introduced on a number of limited trains by W. H. Smith & Sons to coincide with that firm's centenary with British railways.

Pullman kept pace with trends in design from the original plush, garish, florid, ostentatious and opulent Victorian and Edwardian eras to the streamlined Blue Pullmans and the Inter-City cars for the London Midland overhead electrification of the second Elizabethan age. A particular Pullman feature was the table lamp. Each car originally had its own set. The name or number of the car was stamped on the base of each lamp. Shades were of silk. They were replaced by pink, green and white coloured plastic shades. Later, individual sets of lamps were changed in favour of fixed table lamps with white opaque glass cylinder-shaped shades of a standard pattern.

Originally all cars had clocks. It was the responsibility of the conductor to keep them wound and showing the correct time. Many of these were veritable antique timepieces. In due course, mainly because clocks must also be kept in good repair, an expensive process, all were taken out.

Another Pullman feature was the coupé, a compartment for four off a short side corridor. In some third (or second) class cars the coupé seated six, but this was rather a crush. Locomotive-hauled cars were characterised by oval cathedral coloured glass lights in the lavatories. A new type of square window was designed for the 1951/52 cars for the Golden Arrow and plain opaque square glass for the 1960 Eastern Region cars. The first cars were painted a rich mahogany brown embossed with gold leaf. Lord Dalziel changed the livery in 1902 to umber below the waist and cream above up to the cantrail. The umber was later extended to the upper quarter which carried the name 'PULLMAN' in elongated lettering. The roofs were painted white. The cars on the South Eastern & Chatham and the two on the Metropolitan Railway were originally in crimson lake livery. During the second world war those cars in traffic were painted dark brown or in battleship grey. Nanking blue and white was adopted for the 1960 diesel Blue Pullmans and finally umber and cream gave way to BR blue and grey except on the 1966 London Midland cars in 'reversed' livery with silver bodies and blue surrounds to the windows, a livery also worn by the Blue Pullmans for their last years in service. Most preserved cars have reverted to the livery by which Pullman in Britain is identified, though some have remained in their BR colours, and certain liberties in livery have also been taken with cars in preservation.

In the past, at the end of their service, cars were taken off their bogies and converted into dwellings at Lancing, Partridge Green, Seaford and Selsey in Sussex. Several were retained for departmental use, notably the 1900 LBSC *Devonshire*, retired in 1931, and converted into a mess car, and the 1877-built *Albert Edward* used as a store, both at Preston Park works.

In 1960 the future needs of the fleet were re-assessed; 56 cars were retired from traffic, converted into camping coaches at Preston Park and at Lancing and sold to British Railways – 20 to the Southern, 11 each to the Eastern and the Western, two to the Midland and 12 to Scottish Region. These vehicles were originally known as camping coaches, the only time a Pullman was ever described as a coach. The first were painted brown, but this was generally changed later to the standard Pullman umber and cream. In their promotional literature BR referred to the vehicles as holiday coaches to distinguish them from its own camping coaches, and on the sides was painted the inscription 'Pullman Holiday Coach'. These coaches, for a number of years, were a familiar sight in various beauty spots and camping sites served by rail. In time because of the remoteness of the sites, the vehicles proved too costly to maintain; some were even at locations where lines were closed. The project outlived its usefulness and was abandoned, particularly with the development of commercial holiday chalets and camping sites in the private sector. A few survive for use by railway staff.

At the demise of Pullman quite a number of cars were dismantled for their gear and stripped of all fittings. A few stood idle on remote sidings and in workshops, others became departmental vehicles. Some were sold for scrap, others not wanted or condemned because of blue asbestos insulation were incinerated by the special process of a contractor. But even so, a large number of cars have been preserved and they are to be found in various parts of Britain. A few are privately owned, but the majority belong, or are loaned, to railway preservation societies and to commercial organisations.

At one time a redundant car could be bought quite cheaply. Indeed in the early 1960s some were fetching around £1500 when ordinary railway carriages were about £800. The vehicles would be hauled, for the collection of the purchaser, to the nearest railhead. Now with the renewed interest in Pullman, mainly through the preservation movement, a car in any kind of condition commands a high price and there is no lack of purchasers.

The names given to cars always created interest. Originally royal and names with regal connections were used. Later, ladies' names found greater favour. Confusion exists among collectors where names are perpetuated, duplicated, triplicated or quadrupled. There have been, for example, two cars named *Emerald, Falcon, Maid of Kent, Pearl, Rainbow, Ruby* and *Topaz*. There were two *Hadrian* and three *Trianon Bar*s a name selected by Sir John Elliot taken from two small castles in the grounds of the Palais de Versailles. The first was built by Louis XIV, the second Trianon by Louis XV. Two cars carried the name *Cynthia* and *Minerva*. The originals were parlours built in 1924 by Birmingham Carriage & Wagon, put on show at the Wembley Exhibition and afterwards shipped to Italy. During the Exhibition, staff were sent to Wembley to be in attendance. The second *Cynthia* (schedule 179) was a kitchen built in 1925 and the second *Minerva*, built in 1928 (schedule 213), was a parlour brake. In point of fact there were three *Minerva*s, the first, pre-schedule, was built in 1876 as a parlour and sold to the Midland Railway. There could also have been a pre-schedule *Cynthia* for in 1959 a railwayman wrote to the Company for information about an old Pullman car, off its bogies, with two others, used as sheds at Saltley carriage sidings. There were traces of brown and gold livery, engraved windows, a plush ceiling, double flooring, and a name, just discernible, *Cynthia*. It was obviously an American-built sleeper, but after extensive enquiries no record could be found of any pre-1924 car in Britain of that name. So the mystery remains. No identification marks could be found on the other two cars.

Some cars had their names changed in preservation, notably the second class vehicles bought by Bulmer's of Hereford where numbers were altered to names. Car 84 built by Birmingham Carriage & Wagon in 1931, purchased by Ron Ainsworth of the Keighley & Worth Valley Railway Preservation Society in 1966, named it after his wife, *Lorna*. This was also the name of a 1932 Brighton composite car. In Jubilee Year, 1977 *Lorna II* was renamed *Mary*, after the wife of the late President of the KWVRPS 'Railway' Bishop Eric Treacy of Wakefield. Car *Mary* works on the Worth Valley line where it is often hauled by West Country Pacific No 34092 *City of Wells*. This locomotive carries Golden Arrow boards and insignia, a reminder that in the 1950s it was one of the train's regular locomotives.

The Kent & East Sussex Railway actually created a Pullman car from a 20 year old BR unclassed restaurant car No E1955. The vehicle was withdrawn from traffic in 1978 and arrived at the KESR from York in the following year. The acquisition was intended to augment the accommodation on the successful Wealden Pullman and the conversion, undertaken at Tenterden, was also in commemoration of the 150th anniversary of the birth of George Mortimer Pullman. Since 1981 was also the Royal Wedding year of the Prince of Wales to Lady Diana Spencer the car was aptly named *Diana*. Car *Diana* made its inaugural run attached to *Barbara*, on 8 August 1981 on the 19.45 Tenterden Town Pullman 150. Before departure, the author had the honour of performing the naming ceremony. *Diana* is the second car of that name. The first *Diana* started out as third class car No 34, one of the six built in 1891 for the SER by the Gilbert Car Manufacturing Company, Troy, USA which made up the Hastings Car Train the following year. The cars arrived at Ashford in sections as giant kits and were assembled under the supervision of Harry S. Wainwright, then works manager. In 1918 No 34, together with a number of other cars, was bought by the Pullman Car Company from the South Eastern & Chatham Railway. They were refurbished, named and joined the Pullman fleet where they remained in traffic until the early 1930s. No 34 was redesignated *Diana*, given schedule number 105 and entered in the records as a 1919 build. In building and naming a Pullman car outside the Pullman orbit, as it were, the KESR may have created a precedent which other preservationists may emulate.

Several of the pre-1923 grouping railway companies had their own royal train for the Sovereign's use. The Great Western and the LBSC each built a royal train in 1897 for the Diamond Jubilee of Queen Victoria. The Queen, however, preferred her original London & North Western train. Whether the Queen used the LBSC train in her lifetime is not clear but it was used on 2 February, 1901 to convey the dead Queen from Portsmouth to Victoria Station, London, for the obsequies of the monarch in her capital. The LBSC Royal train was scrapped after the 1923 grouping and from then on until the end of Pullman service, when the Sovereign and members of the Royal Family travelled on the Southern, they did so mainly by Pullman.

The original royal car was *Rosemary* a parlour built in 1923 by Midland Carriage & Wagon and normally allocated to the Bournemouth Belle. This car was superseded by *Phoenix*, but *Aries, Aquila, Hercules, Malaga, Orion* and *Zena* were also used, as well as 5BEL sets 3052, 3053 and 6PUL with cars *Ethel, Naomi* and *Peggy*. All were standard cars in traffic and not kept for any special occasions. When required for royal use the cars concerned were taken out of service for inspection, cleaning and repainting or renovation as required either at Stewarts Lane or Preston Park. It was quite normal for passengers to find themselves travelling say on the Golden Arrow, the Brighton Belle or the Bournemouth Belle in a royal car and being looked after by staff who had waited upon the Queen or other members of the Royal Family. At times one or both of the Eastern Region royal saloons 395 and 396, was sent over to the Southern for marshalling in a royal train, or a train for a State visit, for the principals. This was at the request of the Queen. The narrow Pullman vestibules and doors tended to crease the full skirted dresses of the ladies, which were fashionable at that time. The royal saloons had wider doorways with double doors. Originally these ER saloons were built in 1908 for the Great Northern Railway and North Eastern Railway as part of the East Coast royal train. No 395, known as the King's saloon was originally constructed for and used by King Edward VII, while 396, most frequently used on the SR, was the Queen's saloon. It was built for and used by Queen Alexandra and by Princess (later Queen) Mary. Both were handsome and well appointed vehicles. On 26 May 1964 one was formed into what was a decidedly unusual train make-up for the State visit of President Abboud of the Republic of Sudan from Gatwick Airport to Victoria. Headed by electric locomotive No 20001 it consisted of:

Pullman *Isle of Thanet*
LMR Royal Dining Saloon No 499
ER Royal Saloon No 396
Pullman *Hercules*
Pullman *Aquila*
LMR Power Brake No 5154

It will be noted the formation is a strange mix of Pullman, London Midland and Eastern vehicles. The train was crewed by Pullman and London Midland personnel, the LMR restaurant car manager being responsible for his dining saloon and the Pullman Division for its own vehicles. Luncheon was served to the party en-route in the 45 minutes it took to run from Gatwick to London.

In view of the mileage covered, accidents involving Pullman cars were few and far between. This speaks well for the safety of the railway system generally. The older Pullman hands used to speak of the Thirsk collision in 1892 when sleeping car *India* was destroyed; parlour car *Maud* was smashed at Wivelsfield in 1899 (both these cars were pre-1960 schedule) and in the 1927 Sevenoaks crash *Carmen*, one of the SECR cars, (sister car of *Diana* and 1960 schedule No 88) was wrecked.

Both the Devon Belle and the Golden Arrow were involved in minor mishaps. The Devon Belle incident occurred on Monday 22 September 1947 between Honiton and Sidmouth Junction as the up train was passing the down Atlantic Coast Express, each travelling at about 60mph. One of the Devon Belle's steel red name wings on the streamlined boiler casing of the engine – it was a Bulleid air-smoothed Pacific – came off, ricocheting between the trains damaging windows and bodies of the leading two Pullman cars and seven coaches of the ACE. The passengers in the damaged vehicles were showered with flying glass, seven received injuries, but fortunately none were serious. The two Pullmans were detached at Wilton and the seven coaches of the ACE at Exeter. The trains were able to proceed on their way arriving at their respective destinations approximately 45 minutes late.

The Golden Arrow was involved in a triple crash outside Victoria station on 9 December 1949. As the up Arrow headed by Battle of Britain No 34084 *253 Squadron* was entering the station it collided with a light engine, sister Battle of Britain No 34085 *501 Squadron*; at the same time a local electric train ran into the wreckage injuring eight of its passengers. The Arrow passengers and crew escaped unhurt though several were

140

State occasions: 1 – The visit of President Tubman of Liberia on 10 July 1962. The special train is seen leaving Dover Marine headed by Class 71 Bo-Bo electric locomotive No E5015. The Presidential party travelled in the ER royal saloon marshalled third from the locomotive. (*BR, SR*)

State occasions: 2 – The visit of the Shahanshah of Iran on 5 May 1959. The Shah is greeted by HM The Queen and HRH The Duke of Edinburgh at Victoria. Also in the picture is the Right Hon Harold Macmillan, then Prime Minister. Prince Henry, Duke of Gloucester is alighting from Pullman car *Phoenix*. On the Duke's right is Leading Attendant Castle and on his left Leading Attendant Lade. (*BR, SR*)

State occasions: 3 – The funeral train of Sir Winston Churchill crossing the Thames at Richmond on 30 January 1965. (*G. M. Kichenside*)

British Rail's last train to carry the Pullman banner, the Manchester Pullman seen heading towards Euston between Stafford and Colwich on the Trent Valley line behind a Class 86 electric locomotive. (*BRB*)

shaken. The entire train was taken out of service and booked as 'not to go' until a detailed examination had been made. Overnight a replacement train of Pullman cars was collected and made up at Stewarts Lane to take over the Arrow service for the following day. It was staffed and victualled and went out on time.

On 23 January 1948 four Brighton sets were involved in a collision at London Bridge. The 07.30 from Ore to London Bridge, a 6PUL with car *Enid*, was attached to a 6PAN at Lewes, the 08.05 from Seaford with ROV car 1206. The PUL and PAN then proceeded to London Bridge where it collided with a double PAN, including ROV cars 1205 and 1209, the 08.20 from Brighton, standing empty at platform 14. Ten years later, on 25 August 1958, two Brighton sets were involved in an accident at Eastbourne. It was a Monday morning and the 06.47 Ore to London Bridge, a 6PUL unit, had just been coupled to a 6PAN at Eastbourne standing at platform 4 when a steam-hauled train, the overnight Glasgow-Eastbourne sleeper, ran into the stationary electric train. The casualties in both accidents were numerous. Railway staff and passengers were killed, others injured, many seriously. The Pullman staff in the six cars involved in the two crashes were badly shaken and shocked. By a strange coincidence the Pullman in the 06.47 from Ore was *Enid*, the same car involved in the London Bridge crash 10 years previously. Unlike the other Brighton composite-cars, the panelling in *Enid* was in plain oak and known to the staff as the coffin. Certain ships and steam locomotives have had a reputation as being unlucky. Railmen, like sailors, are often superstitious but has there been such a thing as an unlucky Pullman car?

By far the worst accident in which Pullman staff were involved was the disaster at St John's on the Southern on 4 December 1957. In dense fog the 16.56 Cannon Street to Margate steam-hauled train ran into the rear of a local electric train, the 17.18 Charing Cross to Hayes. The Cannon Street train included ROV buffet 7958. The casualties among the passengers were heavy with nearly 90 killed. Miraculously the crew of the buffet car, who were shaken, escaped unhurt even though the car was a total wreck. When an accident occurred the staff's first thought was for their passengers. They themselves may have suffered injury or shock but they would administer first aid and render all assistance possible to the injured until help arrived.

One of the oldest cars still on its wheels is the first *Emerald*, a kitchen car (schedule 32) built in 1910. Towards the end of its life it became a departmental car, redesignated 101, and used as a training vehicle. It was then converted to an LMR camp coach, parked by Betws-y-Coed station and is now preserved. The 12 wheeled 1914-build *Scotia* saw service in the first world war. It ran between Victoria and Dover in a leave train and was reserved for the General Staff. Its passengers included King George V, the Prince of Wales (Prince Edward), and Lloyd George. *Scotia* ended up as a camping coach on the Eastern Region in 1960.

All cars have their histories, but few are as involved as the three-in-one saga of the Trianon Bar. It is a story which typifies the complexities of the Pullman operation let alone tracing the case histories of individual cars. In 17 years there were three *Trianon*s (schedule Nos 250, 68 and 310). The first was a conversion in April, 1946 at Preston Park from the eight wheeled 1928 kitchen car *Diamond* (250). The second was the 12 wheeled third class kitchen car No 5 (schedule No 68) built in 1917 at Longhedge and converted at Preston Park early in 1946. It was a showpiece, for the interior was entirely fitted out by Warerite, a unit of Bakelite Ltd, in grey, pink and cream coloured laminated plastic. The whole car was a bar, there were no supplement seats and it was put into the Golden Arrow just in time for a press trip two days before the re-inauguration of the service on 15 April 1946. On the down trip it disgraced itself by developing a hot axle box. The car was replaced for the regular Arrow service by *Trianon Bar* alias *Diamond* (250). Bar car No 5 (68) was then named (renamed) *New Century Bar* and placed in the London Victoria-Dover Ostend service. However, this car was always intended for the Arrow so in July 1946 it was taken out of the Ostend train, named again *Trianon Bar*, and put back into the Arrow service.

Trianon Bar alias *Diamond* (250), half bar car and with 12 first class supplement seats was renamed *One Hundred* and then *New Century Bar* and put into the Ostend service where it remained until 1952. *Diamond* (250) and No 5 (68) had thus changed places and running names.

New Century Bar (250) was refurbished in 1955 renamed *Diamond, Daffodil Bar* and placed in the Paddington-based South Wales Pullman. When this train was replaced by a Blue Pullman service the bar car went to Eastern Region as a spare for the *Hadrian Bar* in the Tees-Tyne Pullman. In 1964 it was transferred to the London Midland Region and placed in a Euston–Glasgow sleeper but was condemned at York in the following year. With the introduction in 1951 of a new Golden Arrow train set the *Trianon Bar* (68) was replaced by *Pegasus* (schedule No 310) which contained the bar plus 14 first class supplement seats. *Trianon Bar* (68) reverted to its original number 5, as a buffet car and ended its days as a camping coach.

Former Arrow and royal kitchen car *Orion* restored in all its former glory stands as an exhibit at Modelrama, Beer, by Seaton, Devon. Adjacent to the car is an aluminium plaque with a history. The plaque portrays the English and French coastlines with Eros in Piccadilly Circus in London shooting an arrow across the Channel to Paris and the Eiffel Tower, linking the two cities. Originally there were two plaques; the other one was in a symbolic motif of oak leaves to represent Britain and a cluster of vine leaves representing France. The plaques were designed by the son of Friese-Greene, the film pioneer and made by Starkie Gardner & Company in conjunction with the Aluminium Development Corporation, one of the many organisations in which Stanley Adams was interested, and they were presented to the chairman in June 1949. In turn Mr Adams loaned the two plaques to the Pullman Car Company to be put on display in the *Trianon Bar*, the original No 5 (68). In 1951 the plaques were transferred to the new *Trianon* now in *Pegasus*. When this car was dispatched to the London Midland, by which time Stanley Adams was no longer Pullman's chairman, he claimed the plaques still belonged to him and now wanted them back.

Apparently they were never returned and in time the incident as well as the plaques were forgotten.

When Michael Pritchard, managing director of Modelrama at Beer, Devon went to Wolverton to take delivery of *Orion*, where it had been most skilfully restored, he was presented with the Eros plaque, told it belonged to the car, and that it was only cluttering up the shop and he might as well have it. That is how the plaque now in its original spruce condition, came to be displayed at Beer. Make a point of seeing it when you visit the Modelrama. What happened to the other plaque, the one with the oak and vine leaf motif? Was it ever returned to Stanley Adams or is it just collecting dust and tarnish in some rail workshop?

Pullman had its own particular customs and jargon. For example, footstools were known as hassocks, six being allocated per first class car. Each car also had two camp stools for passenger use and a canvas covered one per kitchen for the chef. All cars had runners to be put down at the end of the day's working or when platforms were wet and muddy, to protect the carpets. Chair covers were also provided. Antimacassars were another feature and over the years ranged from large embroidered linen sets to smaller white 'anti's' of man-made fibre with the word 'PULLMAN' picked out in blue coloured thread.

The catering documentation was known as a commissary sheet, a definite throw back to the American origin and a derivative of commissariat. To the office control clerks, the commissary sheet told everything about the food and beverage business done. The restaurant car services did not use the term of commissary; food was called sustentation, abbreviated to 'sust', and drink was known as 'stock'. The railways restaurant car services (on-train catering) carried circuit numbers. This system of numbering services by circuits, similar to that of CIWL, was a good one and in 1963 was adopted by Pullman.

The Pullman train crews were known as attendants, not stewards; the person in the kitchen who did the cooking was a chef, not a cook; each limited train of several kitchens had a senior chef; a conductor was in charge of a train. Much thought went into train formations and in the placing of kitchens. Each one, so far as possible, had to serve an equal number of passengers without undue passing through cars during meal times.

Of the inspectorate there were area and regional inspectors based at the principal stations with an office, and at different times there were travelling and platform inspectors and a chef inspector. Apart from the area and regional inspectors it was found the other inspectorate grades were not very productive and they were eventually phased out through normal wastage. More responsibility was placed upon conductors, leading and attendants in charge. At headquarters, apart from the chief engineer, departmental heads were designated superintendents. There was not a surfeit of managers, the emphasis on responsibility rested mainly upon those who did the work. The Pullman crest was not a badge or a crest, but a coat-of-arms. The vehicles were not coaches or carriages but cars. It is the car which remains the symbol of Pullman.

11 The Staff

THE Pullman Car Company was similar to a regiment. Men joined, served and left, but the regiment went on. Serving members would speak of their former colleagues with respect. They remembered them. Anyone who has served will tell you that Pullman was not an easy company to work for. It was a hard taskmaster demanding a certain standard of conduct, discipline and deportment. You were Pullman. You either loved or you hated Pullman, there were no half measures. The majority who served loved Pullman; it became a part of their lives. Pullman staff were a *corps d'élite*. Long service was more the rule than the exception.

At the beginning staff were recruited from those who had been in service and were not hard to find in Victorian years. In the between-the-wars period the average member of staff joined from school and remained for the whole of his (or, in some cases, her) working life. Some left for other things or to go into business on their own account. Only a few succeeded, some did very well, most came back. It used to be said if you remained two years you would never want to leave – you were Pullmanised. Chef Buckman who had cooked on the cars for King Edward VII was one of the oldest and longest serving members of staff. Well into his eighties he still did a full day's work in the depot kitchen at the stores in Battersea. He died in 1949 aged 86 and still in harness. At Battersea he worked alongside another old timer, chef Watson.

Car *Joan* during the second world war was put at the disposal of VIPs and had a notable crew. In charge was Morice Upstone, who joined Pullman in 1922 from private service and was destined to become staff superintendent, one-time attendant Alf Smith, who later became chief stocktaker, and chef Watson. On one occasion early in the war they conveyed Winston Churchill and his staff to a Channel port. There was an early departure from Cannon Street. Gruffly Churchill informed Upstone he had breakfasted, told him to serve the others and to be quick about it for there was work to do. Meantime he requested a bottle of Port, a large glass and some cracked ice. Later that day just as Watson was about to prepare dinner, the gas failed. But Pullman staff know how to improvise. They broke up some crates and with the wood lit a fire in the gas stove to cook the meal! Apparently the dinner was well received but as Churchill was about to alight upon the return to London he was much taken aback by the chef's appearance. Instead of the usual immaculate whites, Watson was as black as a sweep. Amongst the Pullman staff there was a fund of Churchillian anecdotes. One such was that you never enquired of him if he would like an apéritif – should you have been so misguided you would be the recipient of a growled 'I don't need one, I've already got an appetite'.

With the old Company there was no retirement age. If you were fit and wanted to you could stay on after the normal age of 65. A number would remain on into their early 70s, most with 40 years or more service, and when the time came at last to leave all would say they had enjoyed every moment of their service. Few members of staff were better known than chief inspector Walter Badger who joined Pullman in 1908. In an organisation noted for its discipline Badger was a law unto himself. He was a personality and very priviledged person – he was allowed to wear plain clothes.

Naturally Badger had a fund of stories, his favourite being the occasion when returning from Paris on the Golden Arrow service a passenger handed him a parcel to take particular care of. On arrival at Victoria, Badger gave the passenger back his parcel and was rewarded with a handsome tip. Impressed Badger ventured to enquire if the parcel contained an article of value. It did; while abroad the passenger's wife had died, and the parcel contained her ashes.

Pullman was known for the quality of its catering service. Credit is due here to the many excellent chefs who worked for the Company. There was senior chef Fry of the Golden Arrow who also worked the royal trains, and chef Dalley of the Bournemouth Belle. Both had served in the Army Catering Corps. Nothing ever went wrong when Charlie Fry or Bob Dalley were in the kitchen no matter the menu or the numbers. In the Company's experience the best all-round chefs came from the Services, particularly the Royal Navy. They were accustomed to working in a confined space, were clean, knew how to improvise and were well disciplined. The story is told of a Belgian chef being questioned in the office about a complaint concerning his conduct towards the conductor of the train upon which he was booked. The interview finished and the chef turned to the staff superintendent and assured him he knew what discipline meant – 'I was in the French Foreign Legion'. They say there is a Belgian in every detachment of the Legion.

Hotel chefs used to working with others in large kitchens had difficulty in settling down and dealing single-handed with the varied work on the cars. You had to be good, but versatile. A number of Pullman chefs were self taught and were brought up on the cars. Others had been attendants, which was good for they knew what happened to the food when it left the kitchen.

So far I have written about men but at various times, Pullman employed many ladies on the cars. On the Brighton line there were a number of attractive girls in Pullman uniform when the service restarted after the second world war. Several made good marriages with passengers. For a number of years Mrs Harris was in charge of a Bognor buffet car, and similarly Mrs Eileen Matthews on the Hastings line, where at one time there was an all-lady crew headed by leading attendant Miss Cover. Eileen Matthews joined as a chef and later became a leading attendant. Other ladies worked services to Ramsgate, on the Leeds portion of the Queen of Scots and the Bournemouth Belle. French born attendant Elaine Morley was on the Golden Arrow where she made the bi-lingual announcements over the public address system. For a period there was also a lady chef, Mrs Brown, on the train. Pre-second world war attendants were dressed in a three-piece dark blue uniform with cap. This was changed after the war to the distinctive crisp white shell-type jacket with blue lapels and cuffs, brass buttons and badges, navy blue waistcoats, and trousers with a light blue stripe. With this uniform no caps were issued to attendants. Leading attendants and attendants-in-charge wore blue shoulder cords, while gold cords indicated the rank of conductor. White shirt and collar with a black tie — bow ties were encouraged — completed the uniform.

Lady attendants wore a similar uniform to their male colleagues with the exception of a navy blue skirt with a light blue stripe. Golden Arrow staff wore special lapel badges. The jackets of those on the Queen of Scots, for a while, were faced with a green Scottish plaid. It happened to be that of the Highland Light Infantry a unit in which F. D. M. Harding served in the first world war.

Conductors originally wore navy blue frock coats and trousers. The coats were faced with gold braid. The frock coat was subsequently replaced by a short jacket. Conductors were also issued with caps. The Arrow conductor was issued with two caps, one regular, the other a sea-going type with a short peak to wear on the channel boat for the crossing. Inspectors wore a dark two-piece black braided uniform with caps. Later the braid was omitted from the uniform. As appropriate overcoats and raincoats were issued to inspectors and conductors. The staff superintendent was responsible for the purchase and the issue of uniforms. Everything was accounted for down to the last button and staff were expected to take care of their uniforms just as if they were their own private clothes.

Albert Victor Jones of Raynes Park who joined Pullman in 1919 was the Royal conductor in the years after the second world war. He worked the Golden Arrow when his services were not required elsewhere. The handsome and well liked Conductor Jones died suddenly and tragically on 26 November 1962, at the early age of 57. On the day of his funeral the Southern Region cross-Channel boat *Invicta*, as a mark of respect, flew her flag at half-mast. The other Royal conductors were Charles Castle of the Golden Arrow and Chris Lade from Brighton. Chris Lade, when not needed for a special job, worked one of the Brighton composite-cars or latterly was booked as a conductor on the Brighton Belle. He was the very epitome of Pullman and was also a keep-fit enthusiast. Every morning all the year round, before going on duty, Lade would take a dip in the sea. The Queen was informed of this and whenever conductor Lade took out a Royal train Her Majesty would enquire how the water was that morning.

The last time, on record, Lade worked a special also happened to be the last, of so many, with which Pullman was involved. It was in connection with the visit of Soviet Prime Minister Alexei Kosygin on 6 and 13 February 1967. One train of five cars was used both for the special from Gatwick to Victoria and for the welcoming party from Victoria to Gatwick beforehand on the 6th and the same rake was used for the return on the 13th. The formation was *Phoenix, Carina, Aquila, Perseus, Isle of Thanet*; Prime Minister Harold Wilson MP, travelled each way with Mr Kosygin who on alighting from *Aquila* at Gatwick Airport shook hands with Conductor Lade. E. J. Morris, director and manager of the Pullman Division also travelled on the special trains.

With the variety of traffic the main staffing problems on Pullman cars occurred on the Southern. From a staffing angle the other regions were self-contained and the services, which ran from terminus to terminus, more stable. Long before the term acquired industrial and political overtones, flexible rostering was the norm on Southern Pullman cars. The principal problems, particularly during the summer timetable, centred around the South Western Division on ocean and boat trains and to some extent the special party traffic. For the irregular ocean liner trains adequate notice of each forthcoming weekly programme of arrivals and departures through Southampton (emergencies due to inclement weather conditions excepted) was sent from the SR's superintendent of operations department at Waterloo to the Pullman traffic superintendent who issued instructions to

Pullman staff of timings and make-up of trains. This enabled the Pullman inspector at Waterloo station to augment his cadre of permanent staff with additional personnel detailed by the staff superintendent and drawn from London and country-based staff. When not required for liner traffic the Waterloo-based staff relieved the crew on the Bournemouth Belle. A similar procedure applied to party traffic of which there was usually ample notice of requirements and train formations to assist the staff superintendent's office in providing crews for the cars to meet the specified needs of the particular service. Most of this traffic was cut and dried and comparatively straightforward to staff with reliable personnel.

The staff superintendent had to carry sufficient staff to cover leave, rest days, sickness and standby requirements without exceeding his establishment. For special work the staff office drew heavily on Brighton where services could often be trimmed and where spare crews were frequently available when units were in shops for periodic light or heavy maintenance.

Just as the Pullman traffic superintendent, in co-operation with the superintendent of operations office at SR headquarters, juggled with vehicle diagramming during busy periods, the Pullman staff superintendent similarly had to deal with a jigsaw of flexible rostering. He also had to remember where staff lived so that staff dutied to work specials were able to join their trains, work them and get back home afterwards. This also frequently meant the cancellation of rest days at short notice. The train crews – conductors, attendant grades, and chefs, accepted this and generally enjoyed the variety of work offered by special traffic and other duties, for it made a change from their more regular workings, and provided increased earnings. With the exception of the Leeds portion and the London-based Queen of Scots, staff from other regions were seldom booked for special work outside their own trains and residential areas.

Departmental heads were always reminded by the managing director that the railway was the master and Pullman was a contractor; the demands of the traffic department, which on the Southern was all powerful, had to be met. A typical case was the

Brighton Belle which in off-peak periods often ran as a single unit. The railway often brought in a second unit from Streatham Hill or Lovers Walk (Brighton) at short notice to form a 10-car train to meet a sudden increase in traffic. Staff somehow had to be found. If Brighton could not help and there was no standby staff at Victoria, then some of the crew from the unit already in traffic moved into the second unit brought in from spare. This usually worked, since the staff office saw to it, unofficially, that there was sufficient cover on the Belle not to be caught out. When a four or six-trip working the Belle was usually staffed by one crew through the day, but when the service was augmented to eight trips based at Brighton it became a two-shift duty.

The 6PUL/6PAN crews on the Central Division also worked two shifts. The morning shift usually followed their cars but the late turn tour of duty followed a roster on different cars according to afternoon and evening traffic requirements. Another factor was the long layover time of certain services such as the Night Ferry, a lodging turn, and the Eastbourne Pullman, when it ran, and certain continental boat trains including, at one period, the Golden Arrow. Due allowance was made for cleaning up after the outward trip and again for preparing for the inward or return journey between which the staff booked off. Later with tighter union agreements staff were only allowed to be signed off in the middle of longer layover periods of seven hours or more, which made some of these services uneconomic. Pullman crews generally, and particularly on the Southern, worked hard and it was in reality company loyalty and pride in service which made the intense flexible rostering of Pullman staff possible.

The recruiting of train staff was very selective. New entrants were usually sent out with an experienced conductor who would report on their suitability. The skills of the job were handed down as it were and there were set procedures and drills with most tasks performed by the train crews. F. D. M. Harding, long before the setting up of industrial training boards, appreciated the value of training and in 1948 set up a series of refresher courses for train staff. The school was established in car *Corunna* at Stewarts Lane. In charge was the well respected and experienced Inspector Cullen. In attendance were depot kitchen chefs Horsey and Povey who supervised the work of the train chefs detailed to the course. The syllabus was simple. It simulated a normal day's work on the cars: preparing for traffic, drawing stores, laying up, receiving the travelling public, seating plans and supplement ticket procedures, canvassing drinks, taking order for lunch, serving the meal – here the class was divided into two groups, each one taking it in turns to wait upon the other – billing the meal, cleaning up, completing the documentation of the day's business, ordering stores, strapping up and closing down.

The emphasis throughout was what is now known as social skills. Talks were also given by the various superintendents who were able to deal with any questions. Inspector Cullen proved to be a natural instructor. When not running the school he was assigned to travelling duties. This enabled him to evaluate the training given at the school. Refresher courses were run from time to time with sister car No 101 alias *Emerald I* replacing *Corunna*.

Much has been written in this book about the Brighton Belle and it is only fitting that something should be recorded about its staff. In its final years this busy veteran had five conductors, all original Pullman Car Company employees, assigned to the service. They were Ted Bishop, originally a chef, who made a management grade with Travellers-Fare; Dusty Dunstall, the longest serving; Chris Lade, who we already know; John Verral, and Ronald Turner. The name Harding was notable for there were three with the Company; the managing director, a chef, and the third a maintenance fitter. Tom Harding had worked most services but was longest on the cars as senior chef on the Leeds portion of the Queen of Scots. He was to leave the kitchen to graduate to a management position at Paddington with Travellers-Fare. There were also three Chatfields, all brothers. They came from Brighton, two remained on the section becoming leading attendants with their own cars, the third moved to Harrogate as deputy conductor of the Yorkshire Pullman.

There were two Whyatts. Leading attendant Whyatt one of the longest serving members of staff came originally from Pullman's intrusion on the GWR and remained with the Company. Alf Whyatt joined Pullman as a trainee at the stores, and was to rise to become personal assistant to the managing director. He was awarded the BEM for services rendered, the only member of Pullman, in recent times, to receive a public honour. He was to serve out his time in a management grade with Travellers-Fare.

Behind the façade of those on parade and in the public eye, the uniformed staff, were other members of Pullman, in the offices, stores, the works, and the maintenance men with a roving commission. Again there were the personalities, long service and dedication. Inauguration of new services and the mounting of specials do not just happen, they have to be carefully organised down to the last detail. A tower of strength at all these events was the outside assistant to the catering superintendent, Peter Gower. Be it on the cars or behind the scenes the staff constituted the human side of a great enterprise which contributed to the mystique that was Pullman.

12 The Pullman Organisation

THE Pullman Car Company was sustained by a straightforward organisation with a comparatively small management structure. The objective always was to contain the 'overhead' considered to be unproductive and not revenue earning. There were the offices of the managing director, the secretary and accountant, and those of the five operations departments: engineers, catering, staff, traffic and stores. Each head of department was responsible to the managing director. The secretary and accountant reported to the chairman and to the managing director; he was also responsible, through the departmental head, for all the clerical grades on the company. The works manager and the maintenance engineer reported to the chief engineer. The managing director, chief engineer, and the catering, staff, and traffic superintendents were based at Victoria station in premises above platform 2. The secretary and accountant was in the Thomas Cook & Son building at Mayfair Place, Berkeley Street, but moved latterly to premises at 167 Victoria Street. The departmental heads ran their departments on a very personal basis but always as a team, keeping in close and constant touch with the inspectorate and the services. Communications were good and the main communicator was the telephone. Heads of department were always on call. As a public company Pullman was expected to turn in a profit. This was achieved each year since the second world war. It was achieved by good management, providing an acceptable product and last, but not least, the Pullman supplement.

A speciality was made of the catering service. Catering is an elusive subject. It calls for knowledge and it demands attention to detail. On a moving train it is a race against time. Properly

157

The Pullman Organisation

Christmas Menu

Honey Dew Melon 2/6
Grapefruit Segments Cerisette 1/6
Tomato Soup with Golden Croûtons 2/

Dover Sole Grilled Tartare or Belle Meunière Style 9/6

Roast Dressed Norfolk Turkey with Grilled Mushrooms,
Frankfurters and Bacon
Cranberry Jelly   10/6

Roast Loin of Pork with Dressing and Apple Sauce 10/6

Cold Turkey Ham and Salad 10/6

Château and Parsley Potatoes   Celery Hearts au Jus

Baby Brussels Sprouts

Christmas Pudding with Cream Custard
Oven Hot Mince Pies 2/6

English Farmhouse and Continental Cheese from the Board 2/6

Coffee 1/

Bread Basket of Oven Crisp Hovis and White Rolls
Ryvita and Curled Butter 9d.

Festive season fare 1963 featured on all long-haul Pullman trains running on luncheon and dinner timings.
Menus gave a choice of dishes and of price.

Pullmans for new uses:
1 – Former Devon Belle observation car No 14 stands in Chestnut Avenue, San Francisco, California, used by Western Athletic Clubs Inc as a lounge bar with a built-in side entrance to the main building. Note the British telephone box alongside the car. (*George Comer*)

2 – Pullman Holiday Coach at Marazion, Cornwall, thought to be *Mimosa* of 1914. (*G. M. Kichenside*)

3 – Twelve-wheel kitchen first *Malaga* of 1921, now serving as a board room for Ian Allan Ltd at Shepperton. (*Dr A. Hasenson*)

The Pullman Car Company annual report for 1956 included this photograph of Her Majesty The Queen alighting from *Orion* at Gillingham. *Orion* is preserved as part of Modelrama at Beer in Devon. (*Courtesy Modelrama, Beer*)

CLUB SNACK SERVICE

Fruit Juices :—
Grapefruit, Tomato Cocktail, Fruit Cup   1/–

Hot Green Pea Soup with Croutons   ...   1/–

Omelette and Grilled Bacon 3/9

Grilled Frankfurter and Spaghetti Milanaise 3/–

Cold Collation with Seasonal Salads   ...   5/6

Hamburger, Tomato, Bacon, Chipalata,
          Fried Egg and Sauté Potatoes   5/6

New England Gateau 1/–

Cheese Tray 1/6

Oven Crisp Roll and Curled Butter   ...   6d.

Coffee :   ...   ...   Cup 7d.   Pot 1/2

In any difficulty will passengers please send for the
CONDUCTOR. Failing satisfaction please write to the
GENERAL MANAGER, PULLMAN CAR COMPANY
LIMITED, VICTORIA STATION, LONDON, S.W.1
enclosing your receipted bill.

THIS MENU WILL BE SERVED ON EVEN DATES

Brighton & Kentish Belles, Brighton Composite Cars,
Ramsgate & Bognor Cars

Popular fast food snack service launched on the Southern Region cars, March 1957.

done catering can be remunerative, a fact discovered by preservation societies where a static or a mobile catering service often brings in more revenue than the actual railway side. There are, though, certain limitations as to what can be done on a train. Furthermore catering is performed on a speculative basis for a broad cross-section of the travelling public and often for different market levels. By and large passengers preferred plain rather than exotic or pretentious fare. It was always Pullman philosophy that only dishes which could be cooked and served correctly should be featured.

On most long hauls set meals were replaced by an à la carte service providing a choice of dishes and of prices. On short haul and on commuter services where the passenger wanted something to eat rather than a meal, a snack service (which would now be known as fast food) was introduced. In the 1950s it was a new departure and took time to run in, but once established it met the needs of the market. The change from set to à la carte meals on long hauls also had to be a gradual process of working in. It was not that the staff were incapable, for apart from the ever prevailing time factor, changing the system meant altering deep-rooted working habits which had been boiled down to a drill. But the staff did it and by so doing set new trends in on-rail catering. All menus and tariffs were prepared by the catering superintendent. A representative section of the train staff were consulted regarding any change of policy on the introduction of new lines.

Pullman always kept the initiative and had its own particular way of doing things. Examples include the croûtons *always* served with soup, tomatoes grilled whole, not cut, ginger sugar passed with melon, not the sugar and the ground ginger separately, and the bread basket containing brown and white rolls and crispbread; toasted bacon sandwiches were introduced on the Brighton Belle and Devon cream teas on the Devon Belle. A feature for breakfast on Pullman trains was the silver tray with a selection of fried eggs, grilled bacon, chipolatas (not sausages), tomatoes, mushrooms (the flat type), and fried bread. Pullman also introduced Grilled Gammon Steak Hawaiian, gammon with a pineapple ring, which happened at the time of writing to be the subject of a Travellers-Fare poster. Another feature was Green Peas Illinois, peas (*petit pois* type) and sweet corn kernels. Some foods were considered too highly perishable for train work were never carried such as individual pork pies, crabmeat, plums and made up fruit jellies.

As a general rule all food was freshly cooked on the cars but tests were made with frozen meals soon after this product came on the market in the late 1940s. It was initially a product of J. Lyons & Company with the brand name of Frood. This took the form of a promotion in connection with the launching of the Devon Belle on an introductory trip for the press. On Thursday 19 June 1947, the day before the service went into regular traffic the London based train left Waterloo at 12.22 for a run round the Staines loop when the following Frood luncheon was served:

Tomato Cream Soup

Chicken Chasseur
Parisienne Potatoes   New Peas and Carrots

Orange Mousse
with
Rainbow Ice and Devon Strawberries

Coffee

It was the first time a meal prepared wholly from frozen foods was served on a train in Britain. At that time frozen food was still a novelty, the forerunner of one of the commodities which collectively became known as convenience foods.

The Company flirted with bought-in frozen meals on a few selected services and even went into the possibility of manufacturing its own product. But there was the question of passenger acceptance. Certainly it was not popular with the train chefs nor for that matter with the attendants, and this influenced the passengers. The quality of the early frozen food products was of a high standard though in a straightforward comparison with raw materials it was, of course, more expensive since it was ready prepared. Then there was always that nagging argument of supplying qualified and well paid chefs with ready meals which required nothing more than reheating. Furthermore there was no question of replacing the craftsmen by semi-skilled food handlers. There is no denying that Frood was an interesting product and what it did nationally was to pave the way in introducing and popularising frozen foods on the wholesale (catering) and retail (the housewife) markets.

The stores, sited on the corner of Silverthorne Road and Dickens Street, Battersea, backing onto the sprawling Stewarts Lane sidings and locomotive depot beyond, functioned round the clock victualling the entire Pullman service. With the exception of certain perishable supplies such as milk and bakery lines everything passed through Battersea for redistribution to the London terminal points by a fleet of vans. In passing through the stores everything could be accounted for. All the services converged on the capital and were met with fresh supplies daily. The orders came in from the trains to be transcribed on machines which issued coloured dockets for the various sections of the depot. Orders were made up and dispatched by the waiting vans in their Pullman livery. It all functioned like clockwork. There was also a depot kitchen, a laundry and an accounts office at Silverthorne Road.

Arthur Britton the portly stores superintendent was another character and one of the more formidable of Pullman's personalities. He had joined the company as a boy when the stores were at London Bridge. An indefatigable worker he put in a 12 hours day controlling the entire operation as a very personal affair from a glass fronted office overlooking his domain.

Pullman was a prestige account. Always mindful of that, unproductive overhead accounts were kept to a minimum. The fewer the accounts the less office work was involved. Accounts were carefully selected, requirements specified, there was loyalty to suppliers and accounts were paid promptly. In return no matter what happened the cars had to be supplied and a continuity of service was as important as the quality and price of the supplies.

Most accounts were of long standing. One of the oldest was for tea from Liddell Brothers opened in 1910. Other long associations were with the firm established by Mr Crosse and Mr Blackwell, now part of the Nestlé group, the Nairobi Coffee Company, Carr's of Carlisle, Peek Frean, and Huntley & Palmer for biscuits, and Colman's mustard. Sir Jeremiah Colman, Chairman of Colman from 1900 to 1942 took a personal interest in the Pullman account. Very close were H.P. Sauce and Lea & Perrins (Worcestershire Sauce), then part of the Midland Vinegar Company of which Stanley Adams was a director.

Many of the original accounts have grown from quite small beginnings into very large food manufacturing concerns and such suppliers as the Smithfield firms of Woodhouse Hume, and Peter Duminil, for meat, poultry and frozen foods, Matteson's for delicatessen, Bowyer's of Wiltshire, for bacon and pies, and even Walls Ice Cream have all expanded into national suppliers.

Tate & Lyle supplied the Company with its own wrapped sugar cubes, while Chivers of Cambridge and Coopers of Oxford supplied preserves. Fresh fruit and vegetables came from Borough Market hard by London Bridge station and fish from Janguards of Billingsgate and Smethurst of Grimsby. Other important accounts were with Batchelor's Foods of Sheffield and with W. Brooks of Covent Garden for frozen foods. Bread and bakery lines came from J. Lyons & Company at Cadby Hall.

The drink side of the catering operation was very big business. Pullman was the first to introduce quarter bottles of wine on trains, and spirits and liqueurs in miniature bottles. The wine list standardised throughout the Company was short and representative. A Champagne, a red and a white Bordeaux and Burgundy, and a Hock, all carried in bottles, halves and quarters. A train with constant movement and extremes of heat and cold is not an ideal cellar. The wines on the regular list were selected from those which travelled well. The Champagne was invariably G. H. Mumm Cordon Rouge whose agent, Stanley de Ville, one of the best known members of the wine trade, also had the agency for Bisquit Cognac, and looked after Pullman personally. Other wines were purchased from Bouchard Aîné and Fickus Courtenay. All the well known brands of whisky and gin from the Distillers Company were carried. Other popular selling spirits were Bell's whisky and Ballantine's and Courvoisier Cognac. Three beers were always carried – Bass, Guinness and Worthington. Others came from Simonds of Reading; Fremlins of Maidstone and Flowers of Stratford-upon-Avon, now components of Courage and of Whitbreads. Accounts were also run with Ind Coope, Truman, and Watney.

There was an exclusive supply arrangement with Schweppes for minerals but Vichy water and particularly Appolinaris, possibly the oldest account of all, were always carried. It may not be realised that cigars present a problem on trains. A box of loose cigars would be shaken to a powder in no time by the motion of the train. Cigars had to be packed individually in tubes particularly Havana and Jamaican cigars. The less expensive British cigars are now usually packed individually in transparent foil. Special teak cupboards were provided in cars for the storage of cigarettes which otherwise would either be spoilt by dampness or dried out by heat.

Looking back it is strange how the product market changes. At one time Irish whiskey far outsold Scotch, then little known. Now the situation has long since been reversed. Abdulla cigarettes as a brand was listed exclusively and in three varieties: Egyptian, Turkish and Virginia. In time Abdulla disappeared from the lists in favour of other brands, notably Senior Service and Players Medium, which, for a number of years, vied with each other as the top selling brand. State Express and Philip Morris became the prestige brands.

Crockery came from Dunn Bennett and from Harvey Reed. Then J. Lawley Contracts obtained an exclusive supply. Pullman crockery was made by Lawleys Ridgeway Potteries at Stoke-on-Trent. After the second world war only white crockery was available, since all the decorated ware went for export. Board of Trade permission was obtained to have crockery badged, in black, with the Pullman coat-of-arms for purposes of identification. When decorated ware was again permitted for the home market F. D. M. Harding selected the Biscay pattern of J.

Lawley. With the introduction of the Blue Pullmans it was decided to change crockery patterns and Sir John Elliot selected the Lucerne pattern, again from J. Lawley. After the 1963 integration F. G. Hole, the manager of British Transport Hotels thought it a good idea to change the pattern to their Whispering Grass and it was made by the Ridgeway Potteries for the account. It was later changed for the fourth and the final time by the chief of Travellers-Fare to the standard light green coloured crockery of the restaurant car services. Cutlery and plate were purchased from Lambert & Blaber, Walker & Hall and the Mappin Group. Glassware came from Duralex and the elegant stem glasses from J. Wuidart.

One of the most costly of expendable items was table linen. It had to be washed and often repaired and it also represented an initial capital outlay. The situation was aggravated by the fact that by the time any damp linen reached the laundry it had started to perish. A solution was found in man-made fibres. Pullman went over to Damask Terylene supplied by Finlay Shields and it effected an economy. The product was non-perishable, did not rot, and its only weakness was the fact that it was vulnerable to cigarette burns since the fibre melted. A method was perfected of repairing the cloths at the linen room at Battersea as well as one in the washing and ironing at the laundry.

Large stocks of food, drink and equipment were always held at Battersea as a matter of policy to safeguard against any breakdown of supplies due to industrial action and other hazards of modern society. As a result the Company seldom ran out of anything.

Pullman was expensive to operate and some services were unremunerative but supported by those which turned in an acceptable profit. Always the quest was for additional revenue and one regular source was from advertising. Between the wars Pullman put out a publication called The Golden Way later replaced by the Pullman edition of Londoner's Diary (Reginald Harris Publications). In these publications suppliers were invited to advertise. Promotional literature of all kinds, including book matches and drip mats, were put out on the cars for a fee. The showcases in some of the bar cars were also available for letting and products were also discreetly advertised on tariffs and wine lists, following the CIWL practice, for which listing fees were charged.

During the 1950s and 1960s on the Eastern, London Midland and Western trains running on business timings the majority of passengers were executives on expenses, whereas on holiday and particularly on commuter services the passengers were very cost conscious. There were the regular commuters who took a delight in trying to beat the tariff. Some would go to inordinate lengths to do the Company out of a penny, if possible. For this reason all tariffs had to be drawn up with the utmost care. Once drawn up the drafts were probed for any loopholes, not just on prices but also the wording and the spelling. One slip here and a gossip writer in a daily newspaper could hold the service up to ridicule, the type of vituperative comment which appears from time to time where railways are concerned. Pullman was well aware of the fact no two services were alike and each was treated individually. Standardisation was avoided so far as practical. Menus were changed frequently and endeavour was made, within the limits of on-train catering, to keep all menus and tariffs interesting and the variety of choice adequate. During the author's 21 years Pullman service he personally composed all the menus and wrote all the wine lists and tariffs throughout the organisation. Only occasionally, usually when on leave, was a menu written by one of his assistants.

The feasibility of an inclusive ticket to cover travel, seat reservation and Pullman supplement, and basic meal, as on the airways, was explored when the Blue Pullmans were in the initial planning stage but the idea did not come to fruition. It was however favoured in many quarters and does have much to commend it. Indeed it has featured in some of the Executive services on BR in recent years.

A corridor service to which Pullman was committed on the Southern always presented problems. The service down the corridors and centre aisles was provided from the Pullman — or pantry cars on the Central Division – marshalled in the train. As far back as the 1950s experiments were carried out on the Brighton line with corridor trollies designed and made up at Preston Park, and whatever the works made they did well. The proposal was to send out the corridor attendant equipped to cover not just the first class accommodation adjacent to the car, but the whole train, provided that the corridors and gangways were not obstructed by passengers and their luggage, always the drawbacks of this kind of service. After a series of fruitless attempts the trollies ended up at Battersea depot, hors de combat. The project died the death as impractical. This Pullman first was rather dubious, since, having been tried out, little future was seen for this kind of mobile on-train trolley idea. It was just not Pullman. A more fruitful and profitable idea was a sub-contracting arrangement Pullman had with Walls to sell ice cream on trains during the summer on the Southern. Walls seconded a manager to run the operations, who would engage his own sales staff. Pullman collected a percentage on sales and did well out of the deal.

There were many problems in running a rail catering service. All manner of hazards arose which had to be dealt with quickly and usually by the person on the spot – inspector, conductor, leading attendant or chef. Adverse weather conditions were probably the most frequent cause of delay and disruption with fog, ice, falling snow and floods, possibly frozen water tanks and gas supplies, not to mention mishaps blocking lines causing diversions and cancellations. In the winter timetable all long distance services carried an emergency supply of canned goods, as iron rations, just in case the train got snowed in. The first trains to be taken off in any crisis were the Pullmans and this occurred several times because of fuel shortages to save coal when services were steam-hauled. In any disruption or emergency the first consideration was to get the staff home once they had cleared and locked their cars. When normal services could be resumed they had to get back to their trains with sufficient supplies.

By far the most troublesome of problems were caused to

Pullman by industrial action. It may be threatened or real, but the damage is equal. A threat of a strike or a go-slow and there is an immediate drop in business. Times without number in post second world war years, detailed plans had to be made in the event of a stoppage which did, or more often did not, materialise. Closing down, clearing the cars of perishables and valuable bar stock and getting the staff back to base was often easier than starting up services again. Then there was loss of revenue which did Company finances no good, although work to rule or go-slow action, while irksome to staff was sometimes beneficial to the Company since it often boosted the sale of drink. Some industrial action was indirect but none the less damaging particularly when it occurred on the Continent or took the form of a shipping dispute and boat and ocean train services had to be cancelled or subject to considerable delay. Old Pullman staff often recalled the hardships caused by the General Strike of 1926 and the aftermath of a prolonged coal strike. The longest stoppage in more recent times affecting Pullman services was the one called by the Associated Society of Locomotive Engineers and Firemen (ASLEF) in 1955 which lasted 17 days from 29 May to 14 June. It was almost, but not quite, a total shut down. A few Brighton, Ramsgate and Hastings services on the Southern where drivers were members of the National Union of Railwaymen (NUR), continued to run normally. Pullman was able to staff the cars in these trains which worked throughout the duration. The trains were packed and did good business. The revenue taken helped to compensate for losses elsewhere.

A silent railway and almost deserted stations is an uncanny experience but even more incredible was the way in which the whole system immediately came back to life on resumption of normal working on 15 June 1955.

13 Special Traffic

PULLMAN handled a considerable amount of special traffic, particularly on the Southern. It ranged from private parties to great occasions of state. The former could be anything from a small group travelling in reserved accommodation on scheduled services to special trains formed entirely of Pullmans, or with Pullman kitchen cars interspersed between ordinary coaches, for such events as business conferences, technical visits by learned associations, ship launchings or maiden voyages, weddings, and firms' staff outings. The state occasions covered visits to Great Britain by foreign royalty, heads of state, or prime ministers, the departures and arrivals of our own royal family on tours abroad when sea travel still featured prominently, and royal attendance at events in many parts of Southern England.

All special parties and trains were notified by or negotiated with the railway departments concerned, or through an approved travel agent. Each year between 500 to 600 special party instructions were issued by the office of the catering superintendent whose responsibility it was to liaise with the other departments concerned. For Royal and private specials the railway or region concerned would issue detailed and confidential instructions providing different degrees of supervision and security known as 'Grove' workings on trains conveying the Sovereign, visiting Heads of State and members of the Royal Family on state occasions or 'Deepdene' for other members of the Royal Family when travelling on other occasions. The code 'Deeplus' indicated that the special party was travelling in reserved accommodation on a regular service.

Bowls of flowers were put out in the Royal car together with a selection of newspapers. The seating and the tabling often had to

171

be adjusted to give ample room. A party of senior railway officers always travelled on Grove, Deepdene and Deeplus trains with a Pullman representative.

The Derby

One of the regular Royal specials in which Pullman was involved was that run for the June race meeting at Epsom including the Derby and the Oaks. The pattern after the second world war was set in 1947 when the King and Queen accompanied by Princess Elizabeth, the future Queen, and Prince Henry and Princess Alice, the Duke and Duchess of Gloucester travelled to the Oaks on 5 June and the Derby on 7 June (run on a Saturday at that time). A special train made up of *Plato, Aurora, Rosemary* and *Juno* left from the south end of platform 15 at Victoria at 12.00 and arrived at Tattenham Corner at 12.54. With the exception of 1953, Coronation year, and with the restoration of the Derby to its Wednesday running the Derby pattern was to remain similar for Pullman, although latterly the ER royal saloon has been used. Only the dates, cars and sometimes the staff varied, but not the drill. With the exception of the Oaks in 1957 the present Queen always travelled, but the members of the Royal party would vary. A light refreshment of smoked salmon and chicken sandwiches, coffee and biscuits was featured en-route, and other drinks were available. On the journey from Victoria to Tattenham Corner via East and South Croydon and Purley the route would always be lined by sightseers. When the special passed a school the Queen would be informed so that the cheers of the children could be acknowledged. The return timing of the empty train – it was always a one-way working, varied between a 13.30 and a 14.30 departure.

State arrivals

While most of the specials for state arrivals and departures ran to and from London Victoria there were exceptions, as for example on 28 March 1958 when Pullman provided the Royal train from Shorncliffe at 12.30 to Windsor & Eton Riverside arriving at 14.40 bringing the Queen and the Duke of Edinburgh back from a State visit to the Netherlands. The train was formed of *Isle of Thanet* (parlour brake), *Aquila* (kitchen), *Aries* (kitchen) for the royal party, and *Minerva* (parlour brake).

Lunch was served during the journey:

WINE LIST	*MENU*
Sherry	*Grapefruit Cocktail Cerisette*
Château Latour 1950 *(Château bottled)*	*Grilled Lamb Cutlets with* *Mushrooms & Tomatoes* *Parsley New Potatoes* *Broccoli au Beurre*
Liebfraumilch *Klostordoctor 1935*	*Peach Melba*
	English Country Cheese Tray
Liqueurs	*Coffee*

The wine list offered a choice of claret or hock. Leading attendant Castle acted as conductor and senior chef Fry was in the kitchen.

Old menus are rare so the following one from a Royal train of 21 November 1934 from Dover Marine to Victoria devised by Claude James the then catering superintendent and illustrated on page 174, is interesting. It illustrates the more elaborate fare featured.

Visiting overseas statesmen and royalty arriving in Britain for State occasions normally came to Dover by sea and travelled to the capital by special train. Later during the 1960s with the expansion of air travel they would fly into Gatwick Airport and the special train would convey the party to Victoria, where the train drew up at platform 2 by the royal waiting room (below the Pullman offices) with a vast red carpet across the platform from the principal Pullman. Arrival by sea was more reliable than by air, when standby alternative arrangements had to be made just in case the plane was delayed by adverse weather conditions. On

THE PULLMAN CAR COMPANY LIMITED.

November 21st, 1934

ROYAL SPECIAL TRAIN

Dover Marine to Victoria

✣

LUNCHEON

MENU

✣

CRÈME D'ASPERGES

✣

TRUITE AU CHABLIS
ŒUFS COMTESSE

✣

FAISON RÔTI
CÉLERI AU JUS POMMES PAILLES

✣

SOUFFLÉ AU CHOCOLAT

✣

DESSERT

✣

CAFÉ

arrival at Victoria the distinguished visitors would be met by the Sovereign, members of the Royal family, the Prime Minister, members of the Cabinet, chiefs of the Armed Forces and other dignitaries civic and military. Full military honours at Dover by the Royal Navy or at Gatwick by the Royal Air Force were accorded to the visitors. In the forecourt of Victoria station would be mounted a Guard of Honour drawn from one of the Regiments of Foot Guards with the Queen's Colour, the Band of the Regiment and the Corps of Drums of the Battalion. The inspection of the Guard of Honour was followed by a drive to Buckingham Palace in open carriages with a full Sovereign's escort of Household Cavalry with Standard. The whole glittering ceremonial was usually televised, particularly the arrival at Victoria. A member of the Royal family accompanied by the ambassador of the country concerned would form part of a welcoming delegation and travel by Pullman to the point of arrival. The party would then return to London with the visitors on the special.

An interesting point of procedure with royal trains, state visits and any specials was that the stationmaster, attired in traditional top hat and morning dress, would always take precedence over all present no matter how highly placed any other rail officer present. Stationmasters are now designated managers and the formal gear with top hat is seldom seen.

With certain modifications, but without Pullman cars, the procedure with state visits, the arrival by special train at Victoria, together with all the ceremonial panoply, remains (like the Derby specials) to this very day.

State visits with full honours on what might be termed the standard arrangements took place on 21 November 1950 for Queen Juliana and Prince Bernhard of the Netherlands, and on 8 May 1951 for King Frederick IV and Queen Ingrid of Denmark. Both parties came through Dover with a departure at 13.20 and a 15.00 arrival at Victoria where they were welcomed as guests of King George VI and Queen Elizabeth. The train for the Queen and the Prince of the Netherlands was formed of *Minerva, Ibis, Rosemary,* (for the royal party) *Cecelia,* and *Isle of Thanet. Rosemary* was also the royal car for the Danish party but the other cars were *Aurora, Rosamund, Chloria* and *Juno.* The following menu was served to Queen Juliana of the Netherlands and party:

WINE LIST	LUNCHEON
Bols Gin	*Smoked Salmon*
Tio Pepe	*Clear Turtle Soup*
Pouilly Dry Reserve	*Suprème of Dover Sole Hollandaise*
Château Palmer Margaux 1943 (Château Bottled)	*Tenderloin Steak Béarnaise* *Oven Roast Potatoes* *Braised Endive* *New Season's Green Garden Peas*
Bisquit Dubouché Extra Vielle	*Chartreuse of Fresh Pineapple Parfait Curaçao*
Bols Kummel	*Cheese Tray*
	Celery Cracker Biscuits
La Invicta Cigars	*Coffee*

The menu served to the Danish Royal party was:

WINE LIST	LUNCHEON
Fruit Juices	*Honey Dew Melon*
Sherry Tio Pepe Apetiv	*Hors d'Oeuvre*
Aquavit	*Dover Sole Colbert*
Chablis 1947	*Roast Saddle of Southdown Lamb*
Château Haut Brion 1947 (Château Bottled)	*Jersey New Potatoes* *Minted Green Peas* *Evesham Asparagus Tips*
Evian Water	*Apple Pie & Devonshire Cream*
Cherry Brandy	*A Selection of Cheeses*
Bisquit Dubouché Extra Vielle	*Stuffed Olives Radishes* *Cream Crackers*
Cigars	*Coffee*

All menus for such special events were submitted in advance, through the Southern headquarters, to the Embassy concerned for approval, yet although instructions were given to carry an adequate supply of bottled mineral water because King Frederick, a physical fitness expert, was said to be a teetotaler; this proved to be quite untrue. The King was most indignant when only served with mineral water and wanted to know who was responsible for this false information!

In 1956 Marshal Nikolai Bulganin and Premier Nikita Kruschev of the Soviet Union did not follow the normal arrangements on a private visit to Britain since they arrived at Portsmouth on the Soviet cruiser *Ordjonikidze*. The large party of 60 travelled to London in a seven car train from Portsmouth to Victoria formed of *Minerva, Aries, Perseus* (for principals), *Ibis, Adrian, Carina,* and *Isle of Thanet*.

Already recorded are several occasions when Winston Churchill travelled and apart from his trips in car *Joan* and on the Night Ferry he went by Pullman on several other occasions. When Churchill travelled there was always a sensation, so great was his prestige. He was a legend. He also liked the good things in life. The following dinner served on *Philomel* on 30 December 1952 is typically Churchillian:

Clear West Indian Turtle Soup
Cheese Straws

Dover Sole Meuniére

Grilled Rump Steak Béarnaise
Parisienne Potatoes   Green Garden Peas
French Beans

Fruit Salad
Vanilla Cream Ice

Cheese Tray

Coffee

Wines always had to be available, white with the fish, red with the main dish of meal or poultry, and a liqueur brandy with the coffee.

1953 – The Coronation and Spithead Review

Perhaps the busiest period in the history of the Company was the Coronation and the Spithead Review of the Fleet. Coronation Day was 2 June 1953 but for the railways it began on Saturday 31 May with a 10 car Pullman train bringing official delegations to London. In total on the special and on all regular Continental trains some 20 delegations arrived at Victoria to keep the station staff busy. Pullman's sister organisation Thomas Cook & Son had built a giant 5,500 seat stand on the Coronation route at Apsley House and Pullman had responsibility for the catering. It was a Cook's-Pullman venture inspired by joint chairman Stanley Adams. The stand was fully booked, each person received an elaborate meal box prepared at Battersea stores and supplemented by a running buffet service. Organised by CIWL in conjunction with Cook's was a party of 200 on the Night Ferry as mentioned in Chapter 4 and Cook's in conjunction with Cunard had a party of 500 American visitors to the Coronation brought over on the *Caronia*. This was a Coronation Cruise on Cunard's luxury liner and was a major operation in itself extending over three days. On Monday 1 June an excursion was arranged to the cathedral cities of Winchester and Salisbury with luncheon and tea en-route. About one hundred *Caronia* passengers were carried in a five-car Pullman train.

On Coronation Day the 500 *Caronia* passengers were taken by two 12-car Pullman trains at 04.00 and 04.15 from Southampton to Victoria and conveyed by coach, like the CIWL Ferry party, to and from the Apsley House stand at Hyde Park Corner. The party returned to their ship that evening leaving Victoria at 18.57 and 19.34. Breakfast was served on the morning journey and dinner on the return. The next day, Wednesday 3 June, 125 passengers from the ship were conveyed in a six car train from Southampton New Docks to Dover Marine en-route for Paris.

On Coronation Day the South Western Division of the Southern also had an excursion from Le Havre to Southampton and then by two special trains to Waterloo, each including two Pullmans in the formation for the service of breakfast inwards and light refreshments on the return. The Bournemouth Belle regular working was cancelled and instead it ran to Bournemouth West on a 19.30 dinner timing from Waterloo on the evening of 2 June and returned empty from the West station at 23.10 to Stewarts Lane ready for the normal working on 3 June. Most of the Kent and Sussex coast commuter services were retimed on Coronation Day for an early arrival in town. Some carried special parties, and some regular services were cancelled. On the Brighton side the Brighton Belle, retimed as described in Chapter 4, took a party of 300 from the Brighton Metropole Hotel. Several other parties were booked on the Central Division on both Pullman cars and on specials with ROV catering.

On the Eastern Region the regular Tees-Tyne and Yorkshire Pullmans did not run on 2 June but instead ran as overnight specials for the Coronation. The nine-car Tees-Tyne Pullman train ran as follows:

OUTWARD			RETURN	
Newcastle	dep 23.48	(1 June)	Kings Cross	dep 16.45
Darlington	dep 00.53	(2 June)	York	arr 20.06
York	dep 01.19		Darlington	arr 20.54
Kings Cross	arr 05.34		Newcastle	arr 21.41

A 12 car YORKSHIRE PULLMAN train ran on the following timings:

OUTWARD			RETURN	
Harrogate	dep 23.55	(1 June)	Kings Cross	dep 17.30
Bradford (Exchange)	dep 00.03	(2 June)	Doncaster	arr 20.22
Leeds (Central)	dep 00.33		Goole	arr 20.56
Wakefield (Westgate)	dep 00.53		Hull	arr 21.30
Hull	dep 00.20		Wakefield (Westgate)	arr 20.51
Goole	dep 00.51		Leeds (Central)	arr 21.16
Doncaster	dep 01.40		Bradford (Exchange)	arr 21.42
Kings Cross	arr 05.14		Harrogate	arr 21.56

But the Apsley House stand, the special trains and the other services were not all that Pullman undertook that day, for the Company also provided the catering at four other venues along the Coronation route on premises of travel agents and shipping companies. Yet, however successful the Coronation arrangements, there was no respite, for hard on the heels of Coronation Day came the Review of the Fleet at Spithead two weeks later on Monday 15 June 1953, and sandwiched between these events came the Derby on Saturday 6 June with its royal special.

The operating arrangements alone for Spithead entailed a superhuman effort. Like the Coronation, the Spithead project was spread over three days, that is the day before, the day of the event and the day after. In all the Fleet Review involved 28 special trains, including the four royals, 60 cars and between 9,000 and 10,000 passengers. The catering ranged from breakfasts, dinners, light refreshments to meal boxes. With Spithead coming so soon after the Coronation it meant an intense pressure of work. The whole operation had to be planned in detail, written out, typed, stencilled and issued to all staff concerned, traffic, stores, maintenance, accounts, inspectorate and to the train conductors and leading attendants. Copies of all instructions issued went to F. D. M. Harding, for information. The Chief had to be informed, and he would then select the services he wished to see personally.

The main body of Spithead specials ran from Waterloo to Southampton but some worked between Victoria and Portsmouth Harbour, and one excursion was between Victoria and Newhaven Harbour. The very efficient operating department of the Southern did a magnificent job of work in diagramming the profusion of services. Full credit must also go to those who performed the physical side of the work, the yardmasters, foremen, shunters and cleaners at Clapham Junction, Southampton and elsewhere and not forgetting the motive power personnel. Not only were there the Spithead trains, there was also, at that period, the South Western boat services to be fitted in with a 10-car Cunarder for the *Queen Mary*, the French Line, cruise ships, the Channel Islands and St Malo services. There were also specials during the weekend before Spithead for Lingfield races and party traffic, as well as the regular Bournemouth Belle and Devon Belle.

For Spithead every car was needed. Such was the demand for first class accommodation that a number of thirds had to be declassed. Also with such a large gathering of cars at Portsmouth and Southampton additional gassing, watering, cleaning and light maintenance arrangements had to be made. The main Waterloo traffic, with the exception of the royal trains, was worked by steam trains. The balance from Victoria was handled by electric 4BUF, 6PUL and 6PAN stock. The electric stock was not allocated exclusively to the special traffic and the party timings were written into the working sheets. The stock which took a party down was not necessarily the one which carried them back to London. The following are a selection of the steam services for the Spithead Review.

Admiralty Guests. Trains C, D, F, G, K, L
Six first class trains for 1,800 (300 per train) guests of the Admiralty, Waterloo to Southampton and return with two Pullman cars staggered in each train of ordinary stock for the service of light refreshments.

Train	Depart Waterloo Monday 15 June	Depart Southampton Tuesday 16 June	Cars
L	08.46 (platform 9)	08.46	*Aurelia & Valencia*
K	08.54 (platform 10)	09.32	*Florence & Plato*
G	09.08 (platform 11)	08.53	*Mimosa & Alicante*
F	09.15 (platform 9?)	08.30	*Regina & Seville*
C	09.20 (platform 10)	09.34	*Argus & Ibis*
D	09.24 (platform 12)	09.04	*Clementina & Hawthorn*

The stock workings over the three days 14, 15 and 16 June, of these locomotive-hauled trains shows the complete workings:

Train L	14	Esher spare	
	15‡	05.48 Esher	Staff join at Vauxhall 4 at 06.13
		08.26 Waterloo	
		08.46 Waterloo to Southampton	
	16	08.46 Southampton to Waterloo	
	‡	Waterloo to Southampton	
		18.10 Southampton to Waterloo	Second *Queen Mary* boat

Train K	14	Surbiton spare	
	15‡	06.04 Surbiton	Staff join at Vauxhall 4 at 06.23
		08.36 Waterloo	
		08.54 Waterloo to Southampton	
	16	09.32 Southampton to Waterloo	
	‡	Waterloo to Clapham Junction and back	
		19.20 Waterloo to Southampton	*Flandre* boat

Train G	14	11.45 Southampton to Waterloo	*Golfito* boat
	15‡	08.37 Clapham Junction	Staff join at Clapham Jcn
		08.47 Waterloo	
		09.08 Waterloo to Southampton	
	16	08.53 Southampton to Waterloo	
	‡	Waterloo to Eardley	

Train F	14	Clapham Junction spare	
	15‡	06.28 Clapham Junction	Staff join at Clapham Jcn
		08.50 Waterloo	
		09.15 Waterloo to Southampton	
	16	08.30 Southampton to Waterloo	
	‡	Waterloo to Woking	

Train C	14	Brookwood spare	
	15‡	06.00 Brookwood	Staff join at Vauxhall 4
		09.05 Waterloo	at 06.40
		09.20 Waterloo to Southampton	
	16	09.34 Southampton to Waterloo	
		11.54 Waterloo to Salisbury	
		(not staffed)	
	‡	Salisbury to Clapham Junction	

Train D	14	Walton spare	
	15‡	06.29 Walton	Staff join at Vauxhall 4
		09.09 Waterloo	at 06.59
		09.24 Waterloo to Southampton	
	16	09.04 Southampton to Waterloo	
	‡	Waterloo to Clapham Junction	

Code: ‡ Empty working.

British Transport Commission (Train B)

This ran for a party of 180 consisting of the Chairman and members of the BTC and all its Executives, to join the BTC vessel *Cambria*. They travelled on a seven car train at 08.20 from Waterloo on the 15th, returning at 08.05 from Southampton on 16th. Breakfast was served to the party with 'some suitable variation of the menu' on each of the two trips. The train formation was:

183

	Car	Type	Seats
A	55	Brake	30
B	169	K	30
C	*Philomel*	K	20
D	*Onyx*	P	24
E	249	K	30
F	61	K	36
G	27	Brake	30
			200

The stock was from part of the No 2 Devon Belle set:

14	Devon Belle No 2 12.00 noon Ilfracombe to Waterloo
‡	Waterloo to Clapham Junction
15‡	05.54 Clapham Junction 07.26 Waterloo
	08.20 Waterloo to Southampton
16‡	08.05 Southampton to Waterloo
	Waterloo to Clapham Junction

The English Electric Company (Train E)

A party of 230, headed by Sir George H. (later Lord) Nelson, chairman of the company, travelled in a 10-car composite train with four Pullmans staggered between SR first class coaches from Waterloo to Southampton and return on 15 and 16 June. Breakfast was served on the forward and light refreshments on the return journeys. The train formation was:

K	First	Brake
J	*Sapphire*	K 16
H	First	—
G	*Chloria*	K 20
F	First	—
E	No 8	K 30
D	First	—
C	*Savona*	K 16
B	First	—
A	First	Brake

As can be seen in the stock working which follows, hardly had the English Electric party alighted in the early hours at Waterloo than the train was on its way back empty to Southampton to form an up boat train.

14‡	Eardley to Wimbledon	
15‡	07.00 Wimbledon 07.09 Waterloo	
	07.45 Waterloo to Southampton	English Electric party
‡	Southampton to Eastleigh and back	
16	01.53 Southampton to Waterloo	English Electric party
‡	03.53 Waterloo to Southampton	
	09.53 Southampton to Waterloo	*Andes* boat
‡	Waterloo to Eardley	

Cars *Sapphire* and No 8 had already been in use at the start of the weekend being formed in the Lingfield race train on Friday 12 and Saturday 13 June.

Train A
This was the big 12-car Spithead train. On the 14 June it took the Dilwara party; on the 15 and 16 it accommodated parties for

08.15 Waterloo–Southampton 15 June 1953
BREAKFAST

Fruit Juice   Cereals

———

Grilled Dover Sole and Lemon Wedges

———

Fried Eggs   Bacon   Chipolatas
Tomatoes   Mushrooms

———

Crescents   Toast   Rolls
Curled Butter
Marmalade   Honey

———

Tea   Coffee

three oil companies; additionally on the 16 it again carried the Dilwara party and was then reformed for the up Cunarder, because the Cunard Steamship Company would not accept declassed cars. Over the three days one conductor, 14 attendants and six chefs were allocated to Train A. Fortunately all three oil companies agreed to the same breakfast and dinner menu.

20.35 Southampton–Waterloo 15 June 1953

WINE LIST	DINNER
Apéritifs	*Pamplemousse Cerisette*
	Le Consommé de Volaille en Tasse
Pouilly Fuisse 1949	*Le Homard Thermidor*
Château Leoville Poyferré 1943	*La Selle d'Agneau du*
	Downland aux Pointes d'Evesham
	Les Petits Champignons
	à la Créme
	Les Pommes Nouvelle Olivette
	Les Petits Pois au Beurre
Lanson 1945	*Le Parfait Crinoline Lady*
Moët et Chandon 1943	*Les Fraises de Hampshire*
Coronation Cuvée	
Liqueurs	
	Le Café Double
Cigars	
Cigarettes	

Train was formed:

A	54	Brake	30	Caltex Trading &
				Transport Company
B	171	K	30	

C	Penelope	K	20	
D	Rosemary	P	26	
E	Octavia	K	20	Shell Petroleum Company
F	294	P	36	
G	97	P	36	
H	Cassandra	K	20	

J	Topaz	P	24	
K	303	K	30	Anglo-Iranian Oil Company
L	31	K	36	
M	208	Brake	36	

344 seats

Stock Working

14‡	Stewarts Lane to Waterloo	
	12.15 Waterloo to Southampton	Dilwara party
‡	Southampton to Clapham Junction	

15‡	07.45 Clapham Junction to Waterloo	
	08.15 Waterloo to Southampton	Caltex, Shell and Iranian parties
‡	Southampton to Eastleigh and back	
	20.35 Southampton to Waterloo	Caltex, Shell and Iranian parties
‡	22.45 Waterloo to Southampton	
16	03.41 Southampton to Waterloo	Caltex, Shell and Iranian parties
‡	05.48 Waterloo to Southampton	
	10.24 Southampton to Waterloo	Dilwara party
‡	Waterloo to Southampton	

Train was then reformed for the up Cunarder as by then other first class cars were available:

Montana	Brake	*Rosemary	P
Seville	K	*Penelope	K
*Topaz	P	Leghorn	P
*Cassandra	K	Regina	K
*Octavia	K	Flora	Brake

* from original train A.

187

Charters and Concessions

In 1954 Pullman was invited by a brewery concern to look at a catering concession at a Heathrow terminal building then under construction and which they proposed to back financially. Pullman was occasionally involved in land based catering in addition to its rail operation. However, political implications were a factor in the decision not to proceed but if Pullman had taken this on the whole future course of the Company might have changed. Nevertheless Pullman undertook numerous one-off external catering assignments, mainly in the London area and for organisations in which chairman Stanley Adams was interested such as Bakelite, Guardian Assurance Company, and Thomas Cook & Son. For Bakelite, Pullman looked after its stand at the Farnborough Air Show from 3 to 12 September 1955.

One of the most spectacular external jobs was in connection with the 150th birthday celebrations of Thomas Cook, founder of the great travel firm. It was fitting that Pullman, the sister company, should do the catering. It took the form of three evening receptions for 500 invited guests each, spread over three weeks, on 28 November and 4 and 12 December 1958. The venue was the enormous booking hall at Cook's international headquarters in Berkeley Street, Mayfair, before the core of the organisation moved to Peterborough. The receptions were promoted as a display of international food and drink in which a number of airlines, shipping companies, and overseas travel and tourist organisations associated with Cook's participated. The contributions of food and drink were delivered to the Pullman stores and suitably augmented. On each occasion vanloads of stores with the Pullman staff moved in, taking possession of the booking hall at 16.00 and by 18.00 all was ready to receive the guests. The hall was divided into 30 sections, 25 being allocated to participant contributors, the balance for the dispensing of food and as service bars. Floral displays were also arranged. A uniformed Pullman attendant was allocated to each section and a supply and preparation area was established in the centre of the hall from which the various sections were victualled and the whole operation supervised.

Stanley Adams maintained that an enterprise should expand or stagnate. He was anxious to diversify Pullman's activities within the railway system as well as externally. Diversification led to many and varied projects. Each year from 1954 until 1957 a seven-car train with a bar car (in 1954 observation car No 14, car No 5 in the other years) was sent to Castle Bromwich to stand alongside the site of the British Industries Fair for use as an exhibitors' club. As the train was stationary arrangements had to be made for shore electrical, water and drainage facilities to the satisfaction of the exhibition as well as a very strict local authority. A subvention on takings had to be paid to Pattison-Hughes, the official caterers, and supplies had either to be purchased locally – at a price – or sent by road from Battersea, which proved cheaper. Staff also had to be lodged. It was an expensive operation which whether profitable or not proved to be good for public relations and publicity and bringing Pullman activities to the attention of people who might not otherwise have known about them. Seeing Pullman in action local businessmen started to lobby for their own Pullman train to London. Their wish was granted in 1960 with the Birmingham Pullman.

Quite a considerable Pullman activity was in providing packed meal services for which there was a steady demand from travel agents and tour operators. On two successive years Pullman supplied luncheon and tea boxes for a party of 2,000 children from the Morden and Carshalton area on their annual outing by train to Bognor. Thomas Cook was one of the biggest customers especially in connection with pilgrimage traffic to Lourdes. Cook's had a special pilgrimage department and a representative at Lourdes and each year in conjunction with Wagons-Lits and Pullman, as well as BR and SNCF, organised a number of parties of pilgrims to Lourdes. Some of this traffic went through to Rome. The pilgrims were usually supplied with packed meals on the outward journey and on the return had Pullman cars put into their trains for the service of hot meals.

Where a pilgrimage went out on a Friday special dispensation had to be obtained by the leader if fish, for practical reasons, could not be supplied.

The largest party handled each year was the National Pilgrimage. Meal boxes were delivered to the trains going out from Charing Cross or from Victoria and on 1 June 1954, for example, three special trains, each with three kitchen cars staggered between ordinary coaches ran for the inward journey from Folkestone Harbour to Victoria. Many of the pilgrims were handicapped, some were stretcher cases and were accommodated in ambulance coaches, but there were always many helping hands, Sisters of Mercy, and brancardiers, the special stretcher bearers. This traffic was mainly confined to the Southern though some pilgrimage trains ran through from and to the Midlands. Overall the pilgrimage traffic was quite extensive and although in Britain it was not always handled by Pullman, on the Continent it was dealt with by CIWL.

When Liberace first came to Britain on 25 September 1956 he arrived at Waterloo from Southampton by special train. The Pullman in which the famous entertainer travelled with his entourage had been specially fitted with antimacassars beautifully embroidered with Liberace motifs and piano shaped ashtrays. These adornments had been lovingly made and supplied by his British fan clubs and all disappeared, taken by souvenir hunters, amid wild scenes of adoration from hundreds of women admirers who met the train at Waterloo.

On 5 February 1957 the *Daily Mirror* sponsored the Bill Haley Rock 'n Roll Special for the fans to meet the Rock King at Southampton and travel back with him to London. The train was formed by ordinary stock with *Myrtle* to serve the fans and *Rosemary* for the principals. The chief operating superintendent's instructions read: 'Police control will be required . . . at Waterloo', and concluded with the laconic phrase 'The need for a speedy departure of Mr Haley from Waterloo is essential'. Police control *was* required as the arrival sparked off a near riot. Law and order had to be restored and the station cleared of excited fans before the evening rush hour. Conductor

Coltham, who had also looked after Liberace, described the scene at Waterloo as 'a frightening experience', and it does take a lot to scare a Pullman conductor.

Much football party business was done through Thomas Cook. When a team travelled before a match the request was for a footballer's lunch of boiled mutton, tea and toast. As catering superintendent this request always fascinated me – what was the significance of this particular meal? Train wrecking by football vandals makes national headlines yet Pullman was involved in football specials particularly using the diesel Blue Pullmans on charter by supporters clubs with meal service included in the fare, and there was never any vandalism. Some of these trips took the sets well away from their normal runs as for example Walsall–Bury on 28 January 1967.

Pullman staff were constantly called upon to do the almost impossible, as for example on 15 July 1955 when a GEC party of approximately 400 passengers travelling between Victoria and Erith – a distance of little more than 16 miles – required a catering service. The train on this occasion was made up of 12 first class ordinary coaches with three Pullmans as catering vehicles staggered at intervals. With a departure from Victoria at 10.14 and arrival at Erith at 10.50 coffee and biscuits had to be served in 36 minutes on the outward journey; the return journey was more easily timed and afternoon tea was served in 43 minutes!

There was also the more conventional charter work like the 1954 Bowater annual general meeting trains when three Pullman and one part Pullman train carried 1,000 Bowater shareholders from Victoria to the annual general meeting at Sittingbourne, held in the Odeon cinema.

Pullman charters also featured on itineraries for railway enthusiast groups. The Ian Allan Pennine Pullman on 12 May 1956 was made up of 10 Pullmans, one of the Pullman observation cars and one BR coach to take over 300 enthusiasts from Marylebone down the GC main line and a tour round L&Y routes across the Pennines and back to Kings Cross. It was one of several charters for this firm which often made use of the

191

observation cars and helped to publicise their existence. Alan Pegler, another businessman/railway enthusiast, was a Pullman regular. He chartered several Pullman trains and for several years took a party from Sheffield and Retford to Aintree for the Grand National. A typical working was on 31 March 1962 with car 332 from the Master Cutler and Observation Car No 13.

With the virtual withdrawal from the Southern in 1963 Pullman's special party traffic dwindled. Apart from royals and state visits most of this traffic was handled from then on by regular facilities and services. Under the Pullman Division charters continued on other regions. At the time of writing under its BR and Travellers-Fare management the one surviving train to carry the Pullman name – the Manchester Pullman – still runs Occasionally at weekends the cars were used for charters as we have seen.

But Pullman lives on – if not as an independent trading company then in its preserved cars now in private ownership, many of which are working examples on the privately-run tourist steam railways. They are also running again on BR main lines and this has been made possible for the enthusiast and the general public by British Rail and the Steam Locomotive Owners Association (SLOA) which has a train of Metro-Cammell Pullmans for regular and charter excursions. Then there is the finely restored set of cars running between Victoria and Folkestone as part of Sea Containers Ltd Venice-Simplon-Orient Express venture and on charter work. Through the preservation and leisure organisations the heritage of the past lives again and future generations may see and enjoy something of the standard of comfort, the service and that attention to detail that was Pullman.

Bibliography and Acknowledgements

IT would be difficult to find a book on railways which makes no mention of Pullman. This list thus comprises a random sample of publications in which Pullman has more than a passing mention, many of which have been consulted.

Pullman in Europe, George Behrend, Ian Allan, 1962.

Pullman and Perfection, F. Burtt & Beckerlegg, Ian Allan, 1948.

The Golden Arrow, A. Hasenson, Howard Baker, 1970.

George Mortimer Pullman & the Pullman Company, Carroll R. Harding, The Newcomen Society, 1951.

The Devon Belle, Alan Anderson, Brockhampton Press, 1950.

The Brighton Belle, Nicholas Owen, Southern Electric Group, 1981.

The Bournemouth Belle, Big Four Railway Museum, Bournemouth, 1981.

The South Wales Pullman, G. Freeman Allan, Ian Allan.

History of Pullman Cars, Daily Telegraph reprint, 1929, Pullman Car Company.

A Hundred Years of Pullman, F. D. M. Harding, OBE, Unpublished, 1956.

Mansions on Wheels, Lucius Beebe, Howell-North Press, California, 1959.

Grand European Expresses, George Behrend, Allen and Unwin, 1962.

Cinquantenaire de la Compagnie des Wagons-Lits & des Grands Express Européens 1876–1926, CIWL.

The Restaurant Car, Geoffrey Kichenside, David & Charles, 1979.

The London Brighton & South Coast Railway, C. Hamilton Ellis, Ian Allan, 1971.

The Lost Pleasures of the Great Trains, Martin Page, Weidenfeld & Nicholson, 1975.

Southern Electric, G. T. Moody, Ian Allan, 1980.

On and Off the Rails, Sir John Elliot, Allen and Unwin, 1982.

The Metropolitan Line, Charles E. Lee, London Transport.

Railways of Southern England, Edwin Course, Batsford, 1973.

Railways of To-Day, Cecil J. Allen, Frederick Warne, London, 1929.

Railways of Britain, O. S. Nock, Batsford, 1947/8.

193

Bibliography and Acknowledgements

Railways, Lord Monkswell, Ernest Benn, 1928.
Story of London's Underground, John R. Day, London Transport, 1971.
Steam, John Westwood, Sundial Books, 1980.
The Railway Age, L. W. Cowie, Macdonald Educational, 1978.
Trains Around the World, Octopus Books, 1978.
Kent Railways, B. R. Dyer, James Pike, 1977.
Pictorial Encyclopedia of Railways, C. Hamilton Ellis, Hamlyn, 1968.
The Story of British Railways, Barrington Tatford, Sampson Low, Marston, 1945.

The following journals also contain many Pullman references:
Railway Magazine, Railway World, Modern Railways, Tenterden Terrier, Enterprise (BTH).

THIS book could not have been written without the help and the encouragement of others. I wish in particular to acknowledge gratefully the assistance of the following:
F. D. M. Harding, OBE, former managing director, Pullman Car Company; A. E. Rogers, former field manager, train catering, Travellers-Fare; Doug Lindsay, Kent & East Sussex Railway, for his willing and ever-ready assistance at all times; Doctor Alec Hasenson, MD, London; Leslie Robinson, Greenford, for his motive power knowledge; Roman Schmidt, Reigate, for information on rolling stock and on preserved cars; William Sly, Old Windsor, a dedicated Pullman enthusiast; Christopher Harper, Cuffley, for football information, and Nicholas Owen, Newcastle-upon-Tyne; Murray Brown, press officer North Yorkshire Moors Railway, for information on the 44 Metropolitan-Cammell cars; Moira Hunter of NYMR; S. C. Pritchard, chairman and C. M. Pritchard, managing director, Modelrama, Beer, Seaton, Devon; Alan Pegler, president Festiniog Railway Company; Michael Bayliss, Walton-on-Thames; R. Towell, works manager, Steamtown Railway Museum, Carnforth; Billy Hamilton, public relations consultant and Christine Gutteridge, Project Coordinator, VSOE (Sea Containers); J. B. Cogar, general manager, Dart Valley Light Railway Company; P. Eastman, secretary, Keighley & Worth Valley Railway Preservation Society; British Railways Board; AMTRAK, Washington, DC, USA; George Comer, Daly City, California, USA; last but by no means least to my wife Joan and to my daughter Linda for typing and retyping the manuscript.

Appendix 1
List of Pullman Cars

In Britain from 1915 every Pullman car was given a schedule number in addition to a running name or number. The running nomenclature was liable to change, particularly with those cars built before 1928, but not so in theory the schedule numbers. This list of cars is based upon the schedule of 1 April 1960. It does not include pre-schedule cars. In the 1960 schedule there were some discrepancies and a few clerical errors of dates and names, but these have been corrected as far as possible.

It will be noted some names and numbers have been altered by other designations when the vehicles concerned were converted. Pullman did most of its own conversions. Somewhere in the text it is said that every car has a history. Imagine the size of a book which would contain all these individual case histories. But what a research project it would make if it were possible to trace every single car.

Schedule Number	Date of Building	Running Name/Number	Type	Builder & Notes
1	1876	*Louise*	P	Built USA, assembled at Derby, MR
2	1877	*Beatrice*	P	Built USA, assembled at Derby, MR. Formerly *Globe*
3	1883	*Balmoral*	S	Built USA, assembled at Derby, MR. To Highland Railway. Seaford dwelling
4	1883	*Dunrobin*	S	Built USA, assembled at Derby, MR. Renamed *Culross* in 1888. To Highland Railway. Seaford dwelling
5	1888	*Prince*	Buf	USA built, LBSCR assembled at Brighton
6	1888	*Princess*	P	USA built, LBSCR assembled Brighton. Partridge Green dwelling
7	1888	*Albert Victor*	P	USA built, LBSCR assembled at Brighton
8	1890	*Duchess of Albany*	Buf	USA built, LBSCR assembled at Brighton. Partridge Green dwelling

Appendix 1

Schedule Number	Date of Building	Running Name/Number	Type	Builder & Notes
9	1890	*Duchess of Fife*	Buf	USA built, LBSCR assembled at Brighton
10	1890	*Empress*	Buf	USA built, LBSCR assembled at Brighton
11	1893	*Pavilion*	Buf	USA built, LBSCR assembled at Brighton
12	1893	*Princess Mary*	Buf	USA built, LBSCR assembled at Brighton
13	1893	*Duchess of Connaught*	Buf	USA built, LSWR assembled at Eastleigh
14	1893	*Princess Margaret*	Buf	USA built, assembled at Eastleigh by LSWR
15	1893	*Car No 18*	P	USA built, LBSCR assembled at Brighton. Renamed in 1921 from *Prince Regent*
16	1895	*Car No. 19(I)*	P	USA built, LBSCR assembled at Brighton. Renamed in 1915 from *Princess of Wales*
17	1895	*Car No 17(I)*	K	USA built, LBSCR assembled at Brighton. Renamed in 1915 from *Duchess of York*
18	1899	*Waldemar*	Buf	Built at Brighton for LBSCR. 12 wheeled. Renamed from *The Chichester*
19	1899	*Majestic*	Buf	Built at Brighton for LBSCR. 12 wheeled. Renamed from *The Arundel*
20	1900	*Devonshire*	Buf	USA built, LBSCR assembled Brighton. Mess car at Pullman works Preston Park. 12 wheeled
21	1906	*Duchess of Norfolk*	Buf	USA built, assembled Brighton, LBSCR. 12 wheeled
22	1906	*Princess Ena*	Buf	Last USA built cars on
23	1906	*Princess Patricia*	Buf	British railways for Pullman Company
24	1908	*Verona*	Bke	
25	1908	*Belgravia*	P	Metropolitan Carriage &
26	1908	*Bessborough*	P	Wagon Company
27	1908	*Cleopatria*	P	12 wheeled
28	1908	*Princess Helen*	P	
29	1908	*Alberta*	Bke	First British built Pullman cars
30	1908	*Grosvenor*	Buf	Cravens Limited. 12 wheeled
31	1911	*Vivienne*	P	Cravens Limited. 12 wheeled

Appendix 1

Schedule Number	Date of Building	Running Name/Number	Type	Builder & Notes
32	1910	*Emerald (I)*	K	Birmingham Carriage & Wagon Company. Pullman departmental (training car) No 101
33	1910	*Galatea*	K	Birmingham Carriage & Wagon Company
34	1910	*Mayflower*	K	Metropolitan Railway cars
35	1910	*Corunna*	K	Birmingham Carriage & Wagon Company
36	1910	*Florence*	K	Birmingham Carriage & Wagon Company
37	1910	*Savona*	K	Birmingham Carriage & Wagon Company
38	1910	*Sorrento*	K	Birmingham Carriage & Wagon Company
39	1910	*Valencia*	K	Birmingham Carriage & Wagon Company
40	1910	*Clementina*	K	Birmingham Carriage & Wagon Company
41	1910	*Leghorn*	P	Cravens Limited
42	1910	*Regina*	K	Birmingham Carriage & Wagon Company
43	1910	*Sapphire*	K	Birmingham Carriage & Wagon Company. Loaned to NAAFI in second world war
44	1910	*Palermo*	K	Birmingham Carriage & Wagon Company. Loaned to NAAFI in second world war
45	1912	*Seville*	K	Cravens Limited. Loaned to NAAFI in second world war
46	1911	*Myrtle*	Buf	Metropolitan Carriage & Wagon Company. 12 wheeled
47	1912	*Alicante*	K	Cravens Limited
48	1912	*Rainbow (II)*	K	Cravens Limited. Renamed from *Cosmo Bonsor* in 1948
49	1914	*Glencoe*	P	Cravens Limited. 12 wheeled
50	1914	*Mimosa*	K	Birmingham Carriage & Wagon Company
51	1914	*Hibernia*	K	Cravens Limited. 12 wheeled
52	1914	*Lass O'Gowrie*	Buf	Cravens Limited. 12 wheeled
53	1914	*Orpheus*	K	Cravens Limited. 12 wheeled
54	1914	*Scotia*	K	Cravens Limited. 12 wheeled. First world war VIP car
55	1914	*Mary Hamilton*	Buf	Cravens Limited. 12 wheeled

Appendix 1

Schedule Number	Date of Building	Running Name/Number	Type	Builder & Notes
56	1914	*Ruby (I)*	K	Birmingham Carriage & Wagon Company
57	1914	*Mary Beaton*	Buf	Cravens Limited. 12 wheeled
58	1914	*Daphne*	K	Birmingham Carriage & Wagon Company
59	1914	*Topaz (I)*	P	Birmingham Carriage & Wagon Company
60	1914	*Hawthorn*	K	Birmingham Carriage & Wagon Company
61	1914	*Flora MacDonald*	D	Cravens Limited. 12 wheeled
62	1914	*Fair Maid of Perth*	D	Cravens Limited. 12 wheeled
63	1914	*Annie Laurie*	K	Cravens Limited. 12 wheeled
64	1914	*Mary Seaton*	K	Cravens Limited. 12 wheeled
65	1914	*Maid of Morven*	K	Cravens Limited. Observation car with kitchen
66	1914	*Helen MacGregor*	K	Cravens Limited. 12 wheeled
67	1914	*Mary Carmichael*	K	Cravens Limited. 12 wheeled
68	1917	*Car No 5*	Bar	Pullman Longhedge. 12 wheeled *Trianon Bar* conversion in 1947
69	1917	*Car No 6*	K	Pullman Longhedge. 12 wheeled
70	1917	*Car No 7*	K	Pullman Longhedge. 12 wheeled
71	1917	*Car No 8*	K	Pullman Longhedge. 12 wheeled
72	1875	*Car No 1*	P	Built in USA assembled at Derby, MR. Renamed in 1918 from *Jupiter*
73	1881	*Car No 2*	K	Built in USA assembled at Derby, MR. Renamed in 1918 from *Victoria*
74	1877	*Car No 3*	P	Built in USA assembled at Derby, MR. Renamed in 1918 from *Alexandra* (I)
75	1877	*Car No 4*	P	Built in USA assembled at Derby, MR. Renamed in 1918 from *Albert Edward*
76	1890	*Car No 9*	K	Built in USA & LBSCR works Brighton in 1890. Renamed from *The Queen* in 1918

Appendix 1

Schedule Number	Date of Building	Running Name/Number	Type	Builder & Notes
77	1895	*Car No 10*	Buf	Built in USA & LBSCR works Brighton in 1895. Renamed from *Her Majesty* in 1918
78	1911	*Duchess of Gordon*	D	Built by Birmingham Carriage & Wagon Company. Converted from *Shamrock* in 1927. 12 wheeled
79	1897	*Tulip*	P	Built by the Jackson & Sharp Company of Wilmington, Delaware, USA for SER. Modified 1919
80	1897	*Dorothy*	P	Built by Metropolitan Carriage & Wagon Company for SER. Modified 1919
81	1897	*Thistle*	P	Built by Metropolitan Carriage & Wagon Company for SER. Modified 1919
82	1897	*Hilda*	K	Built by Metropolitan Carriage & Wagon Company for SER. Modified 1919
83	1897	*Venus*	P	Built by Metropolitan Carriage & Wagon Company for SER. Modified 1919
84	1897	*Dora*	P	Built by Metroplitan Carriage & Wagon Company for SER. Modified 1919
85	1897	*Albatros*	K	Built by Metropolitan Carriage & Wagon Company for SER. Modified 1919
86	1896	*Mabel*	P	Built by Metropolitan Carriage & Wagon Company for SER. Modified 1919
87	1896	*Stella*	P	Built by Metropolitan Carriage & Wagon Company for SER. Modified 1919
88	1896	*Carmen*	K	Built by Gilbert Car Manufacturing Company of Troy, New York, USA for SER. Modified 1919. Destroyed in Sevenoaks crash 24/8/1927
89	1896	*Constance*	K	Built by Gilbert Car Manufacturing Company of Troy, New York, USA for SER. Modified 1919

Appendix 1

Schedule Number	Date of Building	Running Name/Number	Type	Builder & Notes
90	1896	*Figaro*	K	Built by Gilbert Car Manufacturing Company of Troy, New York, USA for SER. Modified 1919
91	1921	*Car No 294*	P	Pullman Longhedge. Converted from *Cadiz*
92	1921	*Malaga*	K	Pullman Longhedge. 12 wheeled
93	1921	*Monaco*	K	Pullman Longhedge. 12 wheeled
94	1921	*Neptune*	K	Pullman Longhedge. 12 wheeled
95	1921	*Sunbeam*	P	Pullman Longhedge. 12 wheeled
96	1921	*Car No 96*	P	Pullman Longhedge. 12 wheeled. Converted from *Sylvia*
97	1921	*Car No 97*	P	Birmingham Carriage & Wagon Company. 12 wheeled. Converted from *Calais*
98	1921	*Car No 98*	P	Birmingham Carriage & Wagon Company. 12 wheeled. Converted from *Milan*
99	1920	*Car No 99*	Bke	Birmingham Carriage & Wagon Company. 12 wheeled. Converted from *Padua* a kitchen to parlour brake
100	1921	*Palmyra*	K	Birmingham Carriage & Wagon Company. 12 wheeled
101	1920	*Portia*	K	Birmingham Carriage & Wagon Company. 12 wheeled
102	1921	*Rosalind*	K	Birmingham Carriage & Wagon Company. 12 wheeled. Loaned to NAAFI in second world war
103	1891	*Dolphin*	P	Built by Gilbert Car Manufacturing Company of Troy, New York, USA for SER. Modified 1919
104	1891	*Falcon (I)*	P	Built by Gilbert Car Manufacturing Company of Troy, New York, USA for SER. Modified 1919
105	1891	*Diana*	K	Built by Gilbert Car Manufacturing Company of Troy, New York, USA for SER. Modified 1919
106	1920	*Car No 47*	D	Clayton Wagons. 12 wheeled
107	1920	*Car No 57*	D	Clayton Wagons. 12 wheeled
108	1921	*Car No 94*	Bke	Clayton Wagons. 12 wheeled. Converted from *Ansonia*

Schedule Number	Date of Building	Running Name/Number	Type	Builder & Notes
109	1921	*Car No 95*	Bke	Clayton Wagons. 12 wheeled. Converted from *Arcadia*
110	1920	*Car No 46*	Bke	Clayton Wagons. 12 wheeled
111	1918	*Car No 11*	Bke	Built by LNWR as ambulance coach. Rebuilt 1921 as a kitchen then in 1949 as a parlour brake
112	1918	*Car No 12*	K	Built by LNWR as ambulance coach. Rebuilt 1921. Destroyed in air raid, Preston Park, 1943
113	1918	*Car No 13*	O	Built by LNWR as ambulance coach. Rebuilt 1921 as kitchen car and in 1947 as observation car
114	1918	*Car No 14*	O	Built by LNWR as ambulance coach. Rebuilt as kitchen car 1921 and in 1947 as observation car
115	1918	*Car No 15*	Bke	Built by LNWR as ambulance coach. Rebuilt in 1921 as kitchen car and in 1949 as brake
116	1918	*Car No 16*	Bke	Built by LNWR as ambulance coach. Rebuilt in 1921 as kitchen car and in 1949 as brake
117	1920	*Car No 45*	D	Clayton Wagons. 12 wheeled
118	1921	*Albion*	Buf	Birmingham Carriage & Wagon Company
119	1920	*Cambria*	Bke	Clayton Wagons. 12 wheeled
120	1920	*Catania*	P	Clayton Wagons. 12 wheeled
121	1921	*Car No 40*	Bke	Birmingham Carriage & Wagon Company. Destroyed in air raid Preston Park in 1943. 12 wheeled
122	1921	*Car No 41*	Bke	Birmingham Carriage & Wagon Company. 12 wheeled
123	1921	*Car No 42*	D	Birmingham Carriage & Wagon Company. 12 wheeled
124	1921	*Car No 43*	D	Birmingham Carriage & Wagon Company. 12 wheeled
125	1921	*Car No 44*	D	Birmingham Carriage & Wagon Company. 12 wheeled
126	1921	*Corsair*	K	Clayton Wagons. 12 wheeled
127	1918	*Car No 30*	P	Built by GWR. Rebuilt Midland Carriage & Wagon Company in 1922 to kitchen car. Rebuilt as parlour
128	1918	*Car No 20*	K	Built by GWR. Rebuilt Midland Carriage & Wagon Company in 1922

Schedule Number	Date of Building	Running Name/Number	Type	Builder & Notes
129	1918	*Car No 21*	K	Destroyed in an air raid at Preston Park in 1943
130	1914/18	*Car No 22*	P	Built in first world war as
131	1914/18	*Car No 23*	K	ambulance coaches by Lancashire & Yorkshire Railway. Converted at Longhedge works in 1922
132	1914/18	*Car No 132*	K	Built in first world war as ambulance coach by LNWR. Rebuilt by Clayton Wagons in 1921. Converted from *Anaconda*
133	1914/18	*Car No 133*	K	Built in first world war as ambulance coach by LNWR. Rebuilt by Clayton Wagons in 1921. Converted from *Erminie*
134	1914/18	*Coral*	K	Built in first world war as ambulance coach by LNWR. Converted by Clayton Wagons in 1921
135	1914/18	*Car No 135*	K	Built in first world war as ambulance coach by LNWR. Converted by Clayton Wagons in 1921. Converted from *Elmira*
136	1914/18	*Maid of Kent (II)*	K	Built in first world war as ambulance coach by LNWR. Converted by Clayton Wagons in 1921. Converted from *Formosa*
137	1914/18	*Car No 137*	K	Built in first world war as ambulance coach by LNWR. Converted by Clayton Wagons in 1921. Converted from *Maid of Kent* (I)
138	1921	*Alexandra (II)*	K	Birmingham Carriage & Wagon Company. 12 wheeled
139	1914/18	*Car No 24*	P	Cars built in first world war as
140	1914/18	*Car No 25*	Bke	ambulance coaches by Lancashire
141	1914/18	*Car No 26*	Bke	& Yorkshire Railway. Converted at Longhedge works in 1922
142	1918	*Lady Nair*	D	Built by GWR rebuilt by Midland
143	1918	*Bonny Jean*	D	Carriage & Wagon Company in 1922
144	1923	*Lass O'Ballochmyle*	D	Clayton Wagons
145	1923	*Mauchline Belle*	Buf	Clayton Wagons

Schedule Number	Date of Building	Running Name/Number	Type	Builder & Notes
146	1923	*Car No 80 (I)*	Bke	Clayton Wagons, remodelled from No 27
147	1923	*Car No 17 (II)*	K	Clayton Wagons, remodelled from Third Class car No 50 & Second Class car No 1. 12 wheeled
148	1923	*Car No 48*	D	Clayton Wagons. 12 wheeled
149	1923	*Car No 49*	D	Clayton Wagons. 12 wheeled
150	1923	*Car No 19 (II)*	K	Clayton Wagons. 12 wheeled. Remodelled from Third Class car No 51 & Second Class car No 2
151	1923	*Car No 52*	D	Clayton Wagons. 12 wheeled
152	1923	*Car No 53*	D	Clayton Wagons. 12 wheeled
153	1923	*Aurora*	Bke	Birmingham Carriage & Wagon Company
154	1923	*Flora*	Bke	Birmingham Carriage & Wagon Company
155	1923	*Juno*	Bke	Birmingham Carriage & Wagon Company
156	1923	*Montana*	Bke	Birmingham Carriage & Wagon Company
157	1923	*Car No 54*	Bke	Clayton Wagons
158	1923	*Car No 55*	Bke	Clayton Wagons
159	1923	*Meg Dods*	D	Clayton Wagons
160	1924	*Rosamund*	K	Birmingham Carriage & Wagon Company
161	1923	*Car No 161*	K	Midland Carriage & Wagon Company. Converted from *Fortuna*
162	1923	*Car No 162*	K	Midland Carriage & Wagon Company. Converted from *Irene*
163	1923	*Iolanthe*	K	Midland Carriage & Wagon Company
164	1923	*Rosemary*	P	Midland Carriage & Wagon Company: Royal car
165	1924	*Argus*	K	Midland Carriage & Wagon Company
166	1924	*Car No 166*	K	Midland Carriage & Wagon Company. Converted from *Geraldine*
167	1924	*Car No 167*	K	Midland Carriage & Wagon Company. Converted from *Marjorie*
168	1924	*Sappho*	K	Midland Carriage & Wagon Company

Schedule Number	Date of Building	Running Name/Number	Type	Builder & Notes	
169	1924	*Car No 169*	K	Midland Carriage & Wagon Company. Converted from *Viking*	
170	1924	*Medusa*	K	Midland Carriage & Wagon Company	
171	1924	*Car No 171*	K	Midland Carriage & Wagon Company. Converted in 1947 from *Pauline*	
172	1925	*Aurelia*	K	Birmingham Carriage & Wagon Company	
173	1923	*Car No 56*	K	Clayton Wagons. 12 wheeled	
174	1921	*Jenny Geddes*	D	Birmingham Carriage & Wagon Company. Rebuilt & converted from *Nevada* in 1927. 12 wheeled	
175	1924	*Fingall*	K	Birmingham Carriage & Wagon Company	
176	1927	*Rainbow (I)*	K	Metropolitan Carriage & Wagon Company. Burnt out at Micheldever in 1936. Underframe used to build *Phoenix* in 1925 (schedule 302)	
177	1927	*Plato*	K	Metropolitan-Cammell C & W Company	
178	1927	*Octavia*	K	Metropolitan Carriage & Wagon Company	
179	1925	*Cynthia*	K	Birmingham Carriage & Wagon Company	
180	1926	*Car No 180*	K		Converted from *Camilla*
181	1926	*Car No 181*	K	Metropolitan Carriage & Wagon Company for the Hastings Line	Converted from *Latona*
182	1926	*Car No 182*	K		Converted from *Madeline*
183	1926	*Car No 183*	K		Converted from *Pomona*
184	1926	*Car No 184*	K		Converted from *Theodora*
185	1926	*Car No 185*	K		Converted from *Barbara*
186	1926	*Car No 58*	K	Midland Carriage & Wagon Company	
187	1926	*Car No 65*	Bke	Midland Carriage & Wagon Company	

Appendix 1

Schedule Number	Date of Building	Running Name/Number	Type	Builder & Notes
188	1926	*Car No 66*	P	Midland Carriage & Wagon Company
189	1926	*Car No 31*	K	Birmingham Carriage & Wagon Company
190	1926	*Car No 32*	K	Birmingham Carriage & Wagon Company
191	1926	*Car No 33*	K	Birmingham Carriage & Wagon Company
192	1926	*Car No 34*	P	Birmingham Carriage & Wagon Company
193	1926	*Car No 35*	P	Birmingham Carriage & Wagon Company
194	1926	*Car No 36*	Bke	Birmingham Carriage & Wagon Company
195	1926	*Car No 100*	K	Birmingham Carriage & Wagon Company. 5′ 3″ gauge cars built for Great Southern Railway of Ireland
196	1926	*Car No 101*	K	
197	1926	*Car No 102*	K	
198	1926	*Car No 103*	K	Birmingham Carriage & Wagon Company. 12 wheeled. Converted from *Atlanta* in 1927
199	1921	*Diana Vernon*	D	
200	1927	*Cassandra*	K	Metropolitan Carriage & Wagon Company
201	1921	*Jeannie Deans*	D	Birmingham Carriage & Wagon Company. 12 wheeled. Converted from *Columbia* in 1927
202	1927	*Queen Margaret*	D	Metropolitan Carriage & Wagon Company
203	1927	*Kate Dalrymple*	D	Metropolitan Carriage & Wagon Company
204	1927	*Helen of Mar*	D	Metropolitan Carriage & Wagon Company
205	1928	*Cecelia*	K	Midland Carriage & Wagon Company
206	1928	*Chloria*	K	Midland Carriage & Wagon Company
207	1928	*Zenobia*	K	Midland Carriage & Wagon Company
208	1928	*Car No 208*	Bke	Midland Carriage & Wagon Company. Converted from a car named *Leona*, a parlour, to a brake in 1947
209	1928	*Car No 209*	P	Midland Carriage & Wagon Company. Converted from *Niobe*

Appendix 1

Schedule Number	Date of Building	Running Name/Number	Type	Builder & Notes
210	1927	*Car No 105*	K	Metropolitan Carriage & Wagon Company. Converted from *Marcelle*
211	1927	*Car No 106*	K	Metropolitan Carriage & Wagon Company. Converted from *Sybil*
212	1927	*Car No 107*	K	Metropolitan Carriage & Wagon Company. Converted from *Kathleen*
213	1928	*Minerva*	Bke	Midland Carriage & Wagon Company
214	1928	*Car No 59* *Hadrian Bar*	K	Midland Carriage & Wagon Company. Converted and renamed *Hadrian Bar* in 1948
215	1928	*Car No 60*	K	⎫
216	1928	*Car No 61*	K	⎬ Midland Carriage & Wagon Company
217	1928	*Car No 62*	Bke	
218	1928	*Car No 63*	Bke	
219	1928	*Car No 64*	P	⎭
220	1928	*Car No 67*	Bke	
221	1928	*Car No 68*	Bke	
222	1928	*Car No 69*	Bke	
223	1928	*Car No 70*	Bke	
224	1928	*Car No 71*	Bke	
225	1928	*Car No 72*	Bke	
226	1928	*Car No 73*	P	
227	1928	*Car No 74*	P	Metropolitan Carriage & Wagon Company
228	1928	*Car No 75*	P	
229	1928	*Car No 76*	P	
230	1928	*Car No 77*	Bke	
231	1928	*Car No 78*	Bke	
232	1928	*Car No 79*	Bke	
233	1928	*Car No 80 (II)*	Bke	
234	1928	*Nilar*	K	
235	1928	*Belinda*	K	
236	1928	*Sheila*	P	
237	1928	*Thelma*	K	
238	1928	*Phyllis*	K	
239	1928	*Agatha*	P	
240	1928	*Penelope*	K	
241	1928	*Philomel*	K	
242	1928	*Ursula*	P	
243	1928	*Lucille*	P	
244	1925	*Adrian*	K	Built originally by Birmingham C & W Company for CIWL, Italy.
245	1925	*Ibis*	K	

Schedule Number	Date of Building	Running Name/Number	Type	Builder & Notes
246	1925	*Lydia*	K	Returned to UK 1928 and rebuilt by Midland C & W Company
247	1925	*Isle of Thanet*	Bke	Built originally by Birmingham C & W Company for CIWL, Italy and assumed to be a parlour named *Leona*. Returned to UK in 1928 and rebuilt by Midland C & W Company as *Princess Elizabeth*, a kitchen car. Converted to parlour brake in 1950 and renamed *Isle of Thanet*
248	1925	*Car No 248*	Bke	Built originally by Birmingham C & W Company for CIWL, Italy. Returned to UK in 1928 and rebuilt by Birmingham C & W. Named *Lady Dalziel*. Converted in 1948 to TC No 248
249	1925	*Car No 249*	K	Built originally by Birmingham C & W for CIWL, Italy. Returned to UK 1928 and rebuilt by Birmingham C & W. Named *Pearl* (I). Converted in 1947 to TC No 249
250	1925	*Diamond*	K	Originally built by Birmingham C & W for CIWL, Italy. Returned to UK 1928 and rebuilt by Birmingham C & W. Converted later respectively *Trianon Bar, One Hundred Bar, New Century Bar, Daffodil Bar*
251	1925	*Onyx*	P	Originally built by Birmingham C & W for CIWL, Italy. Returned to UK 1928 and rebuilt by Midland C & W
252	1928	*Eunice*	P	Metropolitan Carriage & Wagon Company
253	1928	*Juana*	P	Metropolitan Carriage & Wagon Company
254	1928	*Zena*	P	Metropolitan Carriage & Wagon Company
255	1928	*Ione*	K	Metropolitan Carriage & Wagon Company
256	1928	*Joan*	K	Metropolitan Carriage & Wagon Company. Second world war VIP car
257	1928	*Loraine*	K	Metropolitan Carriage & Wagon Company
258	1928	*Evadne*	K	Metropolitan Carriage & Wagon Company
259	1931	*Car No 81*	Bke	

Appendix 1

Schedule Number	Date of Building	Running Name/Number	Type	Builder & Notes
260	1931	*Car No 82*	Bke	Birmingham Carriage &
261	1931	*Car No 83*	P	Wagon Company
262	1931	*Car No 84*	P	
263	1932	*Ida*	K	
264	1932	*Ruth*	K	
265	1932	*Rose*	K	
266	1932	*Violet*	K	
267	1932	*May*	K	
268	1932	*Peggy*	K	Metropolitan-Cammell
269	1932	*Clara*	K	Carriage & Wagon
270	1932	*Ethel*	K	Company
271	1932	*Alice*	K	Southern Electric
272	1932	*Gwladys*	K	Brighton Composite Cars
273	1932	*Olive*	K	
274	1932	*Daisy*	K	
275	1932	*Anne*	K	
276	1932	*Naomi*	K	
277	1932	*Lorna*	K	
278	1932	*Bertha*	K	
279	1932	*Hazel*	K	
280	1932	*Audrey*	K	
281	1932	*Gwen*	K	
282	1932	*Doris*	K	
283	1932	*Mona*	K	
284	1932	*Vera*	K	Metropolitan-Cammell
285	1932	*Car No 85*	P	Carriage & Wagon
286	1932	*Car No 86*	P	Company
287	1932	*Car No 87*	P	Southern Electric
288	1932	*Car No 88*	Bke	Brighton Belle
289	1932	*Car No 89*	Bke	Cars
290	1932	*Car No 90*	Bke	
291	1932	*Car No 91*	Bke	
292	1932	*Car No 92*	Bke	
293	1932	*Car No 93*	Bke	
294	1932	*Brenda*	K	
295	1932	*Elinor*	K	
296	1932	*Enid*	K	Metropolitan-Cammell
297	1932	*Grace*	K	Carriage & Wagon Company
298	1932	*Iris*	K	Southern Electric
299	1932	*Joyce*	K	Brighton Composite Cars
300	1932	*Rita*	K	
301	1951	*Perseus*	P	Birmingham Carriage & Wagon Company

Appendix 1

Schedule Number	Date of Building	Running Name/Number	Type	Builder & Notes
302	1952	*Phoenix*	P	⎫
303	1952	*Car No 303*	K	⎬ Pullman, Preston Park
304	1952	*Aries*	K	⎭
305	1951	*Aquila*	K	⎫
306	1951	*Orion*	K	⎪
307	1951	*Carina*	K	Birmingham Carriage &
308	1951	*Cygnus*	P	Wagon Company
309	1951	*Hercules*	P	⎪
310	1951	*Pegasus (Trianon Bar).*	P	⎭
311	1960	*Eagle*	K	⎫
312	1960	*Falcon (II)*	K	
313	1960	*Finch*	K	
314	1960	*Hawk*	K	
315	1960	*Heron*	K	
316	1960	*Magpie*	K	
317	1960	*Raven*	K	
318	1960	*Robin*	K	
319	1960	*Snipe*	K	
320	1960	*Stork*	K	Metropolitan-Cammell
321	1960	*Swift*	K	Carriage & Wagon Company
322	1960	*Thrush*	K	Known as the 1960
323	1960	*Wren*	K	44 Metro-Camm Cars
324	1960	*Amber*	P	(311–354)
325	1960	*Amethyst*	P	
326	1960	*Emerald (II)*	P	
327	1960	*Garnet*	P	
328	1960	*Opal*	P	
329	1960	*Pearl (II)*	P	
330	1960	*Ruby (II)*	P	
331	1960	*Topaz (II)*	P	
332	1960	*Car No 332*	K	
333	1960	*Car No 333*	K	
334	1960	*Car No 334*	K	
335	1960	*Car No 335*	K	
336	1960	*Car No 336*	K	
337	1960	*Car No 337*	K	
338	1960	*Car No 338*	K	
339	1960	*Car No 339*	K	
340	1960	*Car No 340*	K	
341	1960	*Car No 341*	K	⎪
342	1960	*Car No 342*	K	⎭

Appendix 1

Schedule Number	Date of Building	Running Name/Number	Type	Builder & Notes
343	1960	*Car No 343*	K	Metropolitan-Cammell
334	1960	*Car No 344*	K	Carriage & Wagon Company
345	1960	*Car No 345*	K	Known as the 1960
346	1960	*Car No 346*	K	44 Metro-Cam Cars
347	1960	*Car No 347*	P	(311–354)
348	1960	*Car No 348*	P	
349	1960	*Car No 349*	P	
350	1960	*Car No 350*	P	
351	1960	*Car No 351*	P	
352	1960	*Car No 352*	P	
353	1960	*Car No 353*	P	
354	1960	*Car No 354 Hadrian Bar (II)*	P	

Schedule Number	Date of Building	Type of Car & Running Number		Builder & Notes
355	1960	*Diesel 1st Class M60090*		
356	1960	*Diesel 1st Class M60091*	Driving	
357	1960	*Diesel 1st Class M60092*	Power	
358	1960	*Diesel 1st Class M60093*	Cars	
359	1960	*Diesel 1st Class M60730*	Powered	
360	1960	*Diesel 1st Class M60731*	Auxiliary	
361	1960	*Diesel 1st Class M60732*	with	
362	1960	*Diesel 1st Class M60733*	Kitchen	
363	1960	*Diesel 1st Class M60740*		Metropolitan
364	1960	*Diesel 1st Class M60741*	Trailer	Cammell Carriage
365	1960	*Diesel 1st Class M60742*	Cars	& Wagon Company
366	1960	*Diesel 1st Class M60743*		
367	1960	*Diesel 1st Class W60734*		
368	1960	*Diesel 1st Class W60735*	Trailer	
369	1960	*Diesel 1st Class W60736*	Cars	
370	1960	*Diesel 1st Class W60737*	with	
371	1960	*Diesel 1st Class W60738*	Kitchen	
372	1960	*Diesel 1st Class W60739*		
373	1960	*Diesel 1st Class W60744*		
374	1960	*Diesel 1st Class W60745*		
375	1960	*Diesel 1st Class W60746*	Trailer	
376	1960	*Diesel 1st Class W60747*	Cars	
377	1960	*Diesel 1st Class W60748*		
378	1960	*Diesel 1st Class W60749*		

Appendix 1

Schedule Number	Date of Building	Type of Car & Running Number	Builder & Notes
379	1960	*Diesel 2nd Class W60094*	
380	1960	*Diesel 2nd Class W60095*	Metropolitan-
381	1960	*Diesel 2nd Class W60096*	Driving Cammell
382	1960	*Diesel 2nd Class W60097*	Power Carriage & Wagon
383	1960	*Diesel 2nd Class W60098*	Cars Company
384	1960	*Diesel 2nd Class W60099*	
385	1960	*Diesel 2nd Class W60644*	
386	1960	*Diesel 2nd Class W60645*	
387	1960	*Diesel 2nd Class W60646*	Powered
388	1960	*Diesel 2nd Class W60647*	Auxiliary
389	1960	*Diesel 2nd Class W60648*	
390	1960	*Diesel 2nd Class W60649*	

END OF 1960 SCHEDULE

1961/62 CONVERSIONS/RENAMINGS TO 1960 SCHEDULE

Schedule Number	Running Name/ Number	Type	Converted/Renamed From
146	*Car No 27**	Bke	*Car No 80 (I)*
161	*Fortuna**	Bke	*Car No 161*
162	*Irene**	Bke	*Car No 162*
209	*Niobe**	Bke	*Car No 209*
248	*Athene*	Bke	*Car No 248* alias *Lady Dalziel*

* Reverted to original nomencalture.

Appendix 1

LONDON MIDLAND REGION INTER-CITY PULLMAN CARS
BUILT AT DERBY IN 1966

Running Number	Type of car
M 500	K
M 501	K
M 502	K
M 503	K
M 504	K
M 505	K
M 506	K
M 507	K
M 540	P
M 541	P
M 542	P
M 543	P
M 544	P
M 545	P
M 546	P
M 547	P
M 548	P
M 549	P
M 550	P
M 551	P
M 552	P
M 553	P
M 580	Bke
M 581	Bke
M 582	Bke
M 583	Bke
M 584	Bke
M 585	Bke
M 586	Bke

No Pullman Schedule Numbers

KEY
Bar – Bar car
Bke – Parlour car with guard's compartment
Buf – Buffet
D – Dining car
K – Car with kitchen
O – Observation car
P – Parlour car
S – Sleeping car

Appendix 2 Pullman Cars
Preserved Cars

Schedule Number	Date of Building	Running Name/Number	Type	Location & Notes
239	1928	*Agatha*	P	Steamtown, Carnforth, Lancashire. Sea Containers Services Limited
304	1952	*Aries*	K	Yew Tree Inn, Thornham, near Rochdale, Lancashire
47	1912	*Alicante*	K	Marazion, Cornwall. Ex WR camping coach
324	1960	*Amber*	P	Severn Valley Railway
325	1960	*Amethyst*	P	Strathspey Railway, Boat of Garten, Invernesshire, Scotland
305	1951	*Aquila*	K	Bulmers Railway Centre, Whitecross Road, Hereford
280	1932	*Audrey*	K	Steamtown, Carnforth, Lancashire, Sea Containers Services Limited
153	1923	*Aurora*	Bke	Marazion, Cornwall. Ex WR camping coach
185	1926	*Barbara*	K	Kent & East Sussex Railway
278	1932	*Bertha*	K	Bluebell Railway. Formerly Mid-Hants Railway
119	1920	*Cambria*	Bke	Kent & East Sussex Railway. Ex BR departmental car DE 960820
307	1951	*Carina*	K	Steamtown, Carnforth, Lancashire. Sea Containers Services Limited. Formerly static restaurant in Lyons, France
308	1951	*Cygnus*	P	Steamtown, Carnforth, Lancashire. Sea Containers Services Limited. Formerly North Yorkshire Moors Railway
282	1932	*Doris*	K	City Industrial Limited. Fonthill Road, Finsbury Park, N4. Stabled at Finsbury Park, Eastern Region, (BR)
311	1960	*Eagle*	K	National Railway Museum, York

Appendix 2

Schedule Number	Date of Building	Running Name/Number	Type	Location & Notes
32	1910	*Emerald (I)*	K	Conway Valley Railway Museum, Betws-y-coed, Gwynedd, North Wales. Ex Pullman departmental car No 101 and ex LMR camp coach
326	1960	*Emerald (II)*	P	National Railway Museum, York
313	1960	*Finch*	K	Severn Valley Railway
175	1924	*Fingall*	K	Bluebell Railway
154	1923	*Flora*	Bke	Marazion, Cornwall. Ex WR camping coach
327	1960	*Garnet*	P	North Yorkshire Moors Railway
281	1932	*Gwen*	K	Colne Valley Railway, Halstead, Essex. Formerly at the Horseless Carriage Inn, Chingford Hatch, London E4
314	1960	*Hawk*	K	BR departmental fleet. AD 13975876. Chester
279	1932	*Hazel*	K	Black Bull Inn, Moulton, North Yorkshire
315	1960	*Heron*	K	Casterton Taverner Motor Inn, Casterton Hill, Stamford, Lincolnshire. Formerly Nene Valley Railway, Wansford Station, Stibbington, Peterborough, Cambridgeshire. Ex BR departmental fleet
245	1925	*Ibis*	K	Steamtown, Carnforth,
255	1928	*Ione*	K	Lancashire. Sea Containers Services Limited. From Birmingham Railway Museum, Tyseley, Birmingham, West Midlands
247	1925	*Isle of Thanet* *	Bke	National Railroad Museum, Green Bay, Wisconsin, USA. Assumed originally to be built as *Leona*, a parlour. Rebuilt as *Princess Elizabeth*, a kitchen car, converted to parlour brake in 1950 and renamed *Isle of Thanet* *
155	1923	*Juno*	Bke	Marazion, Cornwall, Ex WR camping coach
243	1928	*Lucille*	P	Ashford Steam Centre, Willesborough, Ashford, Kent

Appendix 2

Schedule Number	Date of Building	Running Name/Number	Type	Location & Notes
246	1925	*Lydia* *	K	National Railroad Museum, Green Bay, Wisconsin, USA
316	1960	*Magpie*	K	Casterton Taverner Motor Inn, Casterton Hill, Stamford, Lincolnshire. Formerly Nene Valley Railway, Wansford Station, Stibbington, Peterborough, Cambridgeshire. Ex BR departmental fleet DB 975608
136	1914/18	*Maid of Kent II*	K	Kings Lynn
92	1921	*Malaga*	K	Ian Allan Limited, Shepperton, Surrey
Pre-Schedule	1874	*Midland*	S	Midland Railway Centre, Butterley Station, Butterley, Derbyshire. USA built sleeping car
50	1914	*Mimosa*	K	Marazion, Cornwall, Ex WR camping coach
213	1928	*Minerva*	Bke	Steamtown, Carnforth, Lancashire. Sea Containers Services Limited. From Lytham Motive Power Museum, Lytham, Lancashire
283	1932	*Mona*	K	Brighton Belle Inn, Winsford, Mid-Cheshire
156	1923	*Montana*	Bke	Private residence – Barnwell Junction, Cambridge
328	1960	*Opal*	P	North Yorkshire Moors Railway
306	1951	*Orion*	K	Modelrama, Beer, Seaton, Devon
329	1960	*Pearl (II)*	P	Severn Valley Railway
310	1951	*Pegasus*	P	*Trianon Bar* car. Birmingham railway Museum, Tyseley, Birmingham, West Midlands
301	1951	*Perseus*	P	Steamtown, Carnforth, Lancashire. Sea Containers Services Limited. Formerly North Yorkshire Moors Railway
302	1952	*Pheonix*	P	Steamtown, Carnforth, Lancashire. Sea Containers Services Limited. Formerly static restaurant Lyons, France, from 1973 to 1980

215

Appendix 2

Schedule Number	Date of Building	Running Name/Number	Type	Location & Notes
238	1928	*Phyllis*	K	Ashford Steam Centre, Willesborough, Ashford, Kent
317	1960	*Raven*	K	Severn Valley Railway
318	1960	*Robin*	K	North Yorkshire Moors Railway
102	1921	*Rosalind*	K	Steamtown, Carnforth, Lancashire. Ex SR holiday coach
264	1932	*Ruth*	K	Bulmers Railway Centre, Whitecross Road, Hereford
43	1910	*Sapphire*	K	Ashford Steam Centre, Willesborough, Ashford, Kent. Built as a parlour, converted to a kitchen car. Loaned to NAAFI during second world war. Ex SR holiday coach
319	1960	*Snipe*	K	Severn Valley Railway
320	1960	*Stork*	K	Casterton Taverner Motor Inn, Casterton Hill, Stamford, Lincolnshire. formerly Nene Valley Railway, Wansford Station, Stibbington, Peterborough, Cambridgeshire. Ex BR departmental car ADB975609
321	1960	*Swift*	K	Casterton Taverner Motor Inn, Casterton Hill, Stamford, Lincolnshire. Formerly Nene Valley Railway, Wansford Station, Stibbington, Peterborough, Cambridgeshire. Ex BR departmental car
184	1926	*Theodora*	K	Kent & East Sussex Railway
59	1914	*Topaz (I)*	P	National Railway Museum, York. Presented by Henry Maxwell, July 1960. One of the first Pullman cars for preservation
331	1960	*Topaz (II)*	P	Severn Valley Railway
242	1928	*Ursula*	P	The Spot Gate, Mier Heath, Hilderstone, Staffordshire
284	1932	*Vera*	K	M. Amédée Turner, Westleton, Suffolk
323	1960	*Wren*	K	BR research department. RDB 975427 – Derby
254	1928	*Zena*	P	Steamtown, Carnforth, Lancashire. Sea Containers Services Limited

216

Schedule Number	Date of Building	Running Name/Number	Type	Location & Notes
113	1918	*13*	O	Dart Valley Light Railway Company, renamed *Devon Belle*. Formerly LNWR ambulance coach. Acquired by Pullman Car Company and rebuilt in 1921 as kitchen car; in 1957 as buffet and in 1947 as a *Devon Belle* observation car. Sold to MR, then Sc Region – M280/Sc280
114	1918	*14*	O	150 Chestnut Street, San Francisco, California, USA. Same background history as No 13. Formerly sold to Scottish Region as Sc281
194	1926	*36*	Bke	Bulmers Railway Centre, Whitecross Road, Hereford. Renamed *Morella***
157	1923	*54*	Bke	Steamtown, Carnforth, Lancashire. Sea Containers Services Limited. From Birmingham Railway Museum, Tyseley, Birmingham, West Midlands, renamed *Fiona*
219	1928	*64*	P	Bulmers Railway Centre, Whitecross Road, Hereford. Renamed *Christine***
228	1928	*75*	P	The Spot Gate, Mier Heath, Hilderstone, Staffordshire
229	1928	*76*	P	Bulmers Railway Centre, Whitecross Road, Hereford. Renamed *Eve***
232	1928	*79*	Bke	North Yorkshire Moors Railway
261	1931	*83*	P	Bulmers Railway Centre, Whitecross Road, Hereford. Renamed *Prinea***
262	1931	*84*	P	Worth Valley Railway. Renamed *Lorna* and then *Mary*. Renamed twice by the Keighley & North Valley Railway. Remaned *Mary* by the wife of the late President of KWVR, Bishop Eric Treacy of Wakefield
285	1932	*85*	P	The Nag's Head, Mickleover, Derbyshire

Appendix 2

Schedule Number	Date of Building	Running Name/Number	Type	Location & Notes
286	1932	86	P	Steamtown, Carnforth, Lancashire. Sea Containers Services Limited
287	1932	87	P	North Norfolk Railway, Sheringham Station, Sheringham, Norfolk

Brighton Belle — Motor Coaches

288	1932	88	Bke	Swanage Railway Company, The Station, Swanage, Dorset
289	1932	89	Bke	Little Mill Inn, Rowarth, Derbyshire. Renamed *Derbyshire Belle*
290	1932	90	Bke	Nene Valley Railway, Wansford Station, Stibbington, Peterborough, Cambridgeshire
291	1932	91	Bke	North Norfolk Railway, Sheringham Station, Sheringham, Norfolk
292	1932	92	Bke	Brighton Museum of
293	1932	93	Bke	Transport at former Pullman Car Company Works, Preston Park, Brighton East Sussex

Traction motors and other electrical equipment of all Brighton Belle motor coaches removed before the cars were sold.

97	1921	97	P	Marazion, Cornwall, ex *Calais* and WR camping coach
99	1920	99	Bke	Steamtown, Carnforth, Lancashire. Formerly *Padua*. Converted to parlour brake ex SR holiday coach
210	1927	105	K	Pullman Car Restaurant, 26 Kensington High Street, London, W8. Ex *Marcelle*, renamed circa 1964 *Hebe* for Blue Pullman standby train

Appendix 2

Schedule Number	Date of Building	Running Name/Number	Type	Location & Notes
135	1921	*135*	K	Ravenglass & Eskdale Railway, Ravenglass Station, Cumbria. Ex *Elmira* and LMR camp coach
137	1921	*137*	K	Ravenglass & Eskdale Railway, Ravenglass Station, Cumbria. Ex *Maid of Kent* (I) and LMR camp coach. 135 & 137 originally built 1914/18 as ambulance coaches by LNWR. Acquired 1921 by Pullman Car Company, rebuilt as composite cars 1934 and again as third class cars in 1948
332	1960	*332*	K	Platform 1 Public House, Pannal (the old station house), Harrogate, North Yorkshire. Formerly on North Yorkshire Moors Railway. Renamed *Mae*
333	1960	*333*	K	Casterton Taverner Motor Inn, Casterton Hill, Stamford, Lincolnshire. Renamed *Magna*
335	1960	*335*	K	SLOA. Carlisle, Cumbria. Formerly BR departmental car DB975584
337	1960	*337*	K	Casterton Taverner Motor Inn, Casterton Hill, Stamford, Lincolnshire. Formerly Nene Valley Railway, Wansford Station, Stibbington, Peterborough, Cambridgeshire
340	1960	*340*	K	Avon Causeway Hotel, Hurn, Christchurch, Dorset
346	1960	*346*	K	Casterton Taverner Motor Inn, Casterton Hill, Stamford, Lincolnshire. Renamed *Castra*
347	1960	*347*	P	Carlisle, Cumbria
348	1960	*348*	P	Steam Locomotive Operators
349	1960	*349*	P	Association
350	1960	*350*	P	(SLOA)
351	1960	*351*	P	Known as the Carlisle cars since
352	1960	*352*	P	this is where these cars – 347 to 354
353	1960	*353*	P	are maintained by BR

Appendix 2

Schedule Number	Date of Building	Running Name/Number	Type	Location & Notes
354	1960	*Hadrian Bar (II)	P	*Built as second class car No 354 with 24 seats and a bar named Hadrian replacing Hadrian Bar (I) ex Tees Tyne Pullman; ex M354E Nightcap Bar, in Euston–Glasgow Night Limited

NOTES

* Built by Birmingham C & W 1925 for CIWL, Italy. Returned to UK 1928, modified by Midland C & W. Ten cars built for CIWL 1925, eight returned 1928, three are preserved and they are schedule 245, 246, 247.

** Renamed by Bulmer's, Hereford. Names are those of the wives of the directors of H. P. Bulmer Limited at the time of purchase.

Sea Containers Services Limited cars are in connection with the Venice–Simplon–Orient Express (VSOE) project.

Four of the five cars in the Funeral Train of Sir Winston Churchill on 30.1.1965 are preserved, schedule 246, 247, 301, 307. the fifth car 208, ex *Leona* built 1927, location unknown. This car must not be confused with the one of the same name built for CIWL and assumed to be *Isle of Thanet.*

Original designations of camping coaches:
LMR camp coach. SR holiday coach. ER camp coach.
WR camping coach, Sc camp coach.
Later all redesignated: Pullman holiday coach.
The cars at Marazion are used by British Railways (WR) Staff Association and maintained on site by Western Region.

Not all preserved cars are in running order. Some are on wheels and others off their bogies as static display or as a catering vehicle.
Many are privately owned and most cars have changed ownership several times.
Cars in approved running order are subject to leasing and loaning.

Index

Index

Index

Index